CONSUMER and BUSINESS MATHEMATICS

by
Robert Meyer

MONARCH PRESS

ABOUT THE AUTHOR

Robert Meyer is Chairman of the Accounting and Business Practice Department at William Cullen Bryant High School in Long Island City, New York. He was Chairman of the New York City Board of Education Business Mathematics Syllabus Revision Committee which prepared the official course of study "Business Mathematics for High Schools."

TO THE STUDENT

Why You Need to Know Your Math

Throughout your life you will be facing situations that you will be able to understand and deal with only if you know your mathematics. What are some of these situations?

Suppose you have a part-time job in which you will be paid on an hourly basis. In that job you will have to know whether your gross pay is correct, why the cash in your envelope is much less and whether you are paid the correct amount. You will also have to know whether you need to prepare an income tax return at the end of the year; and if so, how you can find the amount of your tax.

Or, suppose your father wishes to buy a new television set. If he does not pay cash, how much more will the set cost if he buys it on the installment plan? How much will have to be paid each week or month? What will happen if your father does not meet the payments?

Or, let us say you own a car or drive your father's car. What does the insurance cost? What will happen to the cost if you have a poor driving record? Will the cost of insurance be less for a girl? Does your age have anything to do with the cost?

These are just a few of countless situations in which you will need to use mathematics.

By means of easy, step-by-step instructions, this book will show you how to understand and solve real life problems with mathematics.

How This Book Is Organized

Each topic provides:

1. *An opening exercise:* A review of arithmetic fundamentals that you will need to know in order to learn new work.

2. *A sample problem:* This presents an actual situation that you will face in life.

3. *An explanation:* Provides information that you need to know if you are to be able to solve the problem.

4. *Sample solution:* The solution is carefully labeled so as to help you understand.

5. *Notes or Shortcut Method*

6. *Additional problems:* These are similar to the sample problem, so as to give you practice in doing new work. These problems begin with those that are simple, and gradually become more challenging as you learn.

After your teacher has taught the new work, read the explanation and see if you can solve the sample problem at home. If you were absent when the new work was taught, read it by yourself, to make up the work you missed.

Robert Meyer

TABLE OF CONTENTS

UNIT 1

Invoicing Skills

SECTION 1   **Buying 10, 100, 1,000 Items**

Class Drill

A. Add down; check your work by adding up.

	1. $ 4.34	2. $14.25	3. $148.16	4. $79.12	5. $158.16
	17.52	8.62	74.00	43.18	78.84
	14.93	.08	36.04	.59	93.25
	.42	.91	36.83	1.48	162.15

B. Multiply; check your work by reversing the factors and multiplying again.

6. 23	7. 163	8. 2.53	9. .85	10. 1.64
×47	×82	×76	×2.5	×1.5

Sample Problems

Problem 1. Bill can buy 10 ball point pens for $.17 each. What would they cost?

Problem 2. If Bill wishes to buy 100 pens at $.17 each, what would they cost?

Explanation

Problem 1: Bill could multiply $.17 by 10, as follows:

$.17
×10
$1.70 Cost of pens

There is a quicker way to do the problem, however. Notice that the answer is similar to the original cost, except that the decimal point has moved one place to the right.

Problem 2: Bill could multiply $.17 by 100 as follows:

$$\begin{array}{r} \$.17 \\ \times\,100 \\ \hline \end{array}$$

$17.00 Cost of pens

Again, there is a quicker way. Notice that the answer is similar to the original cost, except that the decimal point has moved two places to the right.

Notes

> *Use this short cut:*
> To multiply a number by 10, 100, 1,000, move the decimal point to the *right* as many places as there are zeros in the multiplier.

Sample Solutions

Problem 1. $.17 × 10 = $1.70
Problem 2. $.17 × 100 = $17.00

Problems

Find the cost of each of the following:

Group A

Multiplication by 10

1. 10 pens at $.14 each
2. 10 pens at $.18 each
3. 10 books at $1.25 each
4. 10 books at $1.30 each
5. 10 dresses at $12 each
6. 10 dresses at $14 each
7. 10 coats at $32 each
8. 10 coats at $45 each

Group B

Multiplication by 100

1. 100 pens at $.15 each
2. 100 pens at $.21 each
3. 100 books at $1.35 each
4. 100 books at $2.10 each
5. 100 dresses at $15 each
6. 100 dresses at $17 each
7. 100 coats at $35.25 each
8. 100 coats at $43.75 each

Group C

Multiplication by 1,000

1. 1,000 pens at $.12 each
2. 1,000 pens at $.16 each
3. 1,000 books at $1.25 each
4. 1,000 books at $2.20 each
5. 1,000 dresses at $16 each
6. 1,000 dresses at $20 each
7. 1,000 coats at $35.15 each
8. 1,000 coats at $14.19 each

Group D

Mixed

1. 10 pens at $.14 each
2. 1,000 pens at $.19 each
3. 100 pens at $.17 each
4. 10 books at $1.20 each
5. 1,000 books at $1.75 each
6. 100 books at $1.20 each
7. 10 coats at $17 each
8. 100 coats at $18.25 each

SECTION 2   Business Terms: Per M, Per C, Per CWT

Class Drill

Multiply:

1. 7 × 10
2. 86 × 100
3. 5 × 1,000
4. 24 × 10
5. $7.50 × 10
6. $8.45 × 100

2

| 7. $9.72 × 1,000 | 9. $8.52 × 100 | 11. $.75 × 1,000 |
| 8. $22.50 × 10 | 10. $75.30 × 10 | 12. $.24 × 10 |

Sample Problem

Bryant High School buys 4,500 letterheads at $30 per M. Find the cost.

Explanation

Business firms sell some merchandise by the thousand (per M), by the hundred (per C), by the hundred pounds (per cwt). To solve the problem, first find how many hundreds or thousands there are, and then multiply by the price.

The number of thousands could be found by dividing 4,500 by 1,000 as follows:

$$
\begin{array}{r}
4.5 \\
1,000)\overline{4,500.0} \\
4,000 \\
\hline
500\ 0 \\
500\ 0 \\
\hline
\end{array}
$$

Notice that the answer is similar to the original number, except that the decimal point has moved three places to the left.

Notes

Use this short cut:
To divide a number by 10, 100, or 1,000, move the decimal point to the *left* as many places as there are zeros in the divisor.

Sample Solution

$$4,500 ÷ 1,000 = 4.5 \text{ thousands}$$
$$
\begin{array}{r}
4.5 \\
× 30 \\
\hline
135.0 = \$135.00 \text{ Cost}
\end{array}
$$

Problems

Find the cost of each of the following.

Group A

Per M (Division by 1,000)
1. 2,000 letterheads at $25 per M
2. 3,000 letterheads at $35 per M
3. 5,000 letterheads at $20 per M
4. 6,000 letterheads at $15 per M
5. 2,500 letterheads at $20 per M
6. 3,500 letterheads at $20 per M
7. 7,800 letterheads at $30 per M
8. 6,400 letterheads at $20 per M

Group B

Per C (Division by 100)
1. 500 envelopes at $2 per C
2. 700 envelopes at $3 per C
3. 400 envelopes at $5 per C
4. 800 envelopes at $6 per C
5. 550 sheets at $3 per C
6. 650 sheets at $4 per C
7. 730 sheets at $5 per C
8. 640 sheets at $2 per C

Group C

Per cwt (Division by 100)
1. 400 lbs. wire at $12 per cwt.
2. 900 lbs. wire at $13 per cwt.
3. 450 lbs. wire at $9 per cwt.
4. 860 lbs. wire at $8 per cwt.

Group D

(Division by 10)

1. 10 pens cost $1.80. How much would 1 pen cost?
2. 10 pens cost $2.10. How much would 1 pen cost?
3. 10 books cost $35.00. How much would 1 book cost?
4. 10 books cost $42.00. How much would 1 book cost?

Group E

Mixed: Multiplication and Division

1. 6,500 envelopes at $1.25 per C
2. 7,500 envelopes at $1.50 per C
3. 10 books at $1.75 each
4. 10 books at $1.95 each
5. 10,000 envelopes at $17.25 per M
6. 8,000 envelopes at $16.50 per M
7. 100 pens at $.19 each
8. 100 pens at $.21 each
9. 840 sheets at $2 per C
10. 950 sheets at $3 per C
11. 10 coats at $65 each
12. 10 coats at $70 each

SECTION 3   Denominate Numbers

Class Drill

1. Divide:
   a. 350 by 10
   b. 26,000 by 100
   c. 4,200 by 1000
   d. 450 by 100
   e. 75 by 10

2. Multiply:
   a. 85 × 10
   b. 43 × 100
   c. 125 × 1000
   d. 7.3 × 100
   e. 6.25 × 1000

3. Divide:
   a. 6.2 by 10
   b. 7.55 by 10
   c. 125.4 by 100
   d. 12.72 by 100
   e. 1043.4 by 1000

4. Divide:
   a. 434 by 7
   b. $4.68 by 6
   c. $3.92 by 8
   d. $21.33 by 9
   e. 2.768 by 8

Sample Problem

Find the cost of 1 can of soda at $1.00 per dozen.

Explanation

You must know that there are 12 cans in a dozen. When buying in a retail store any fraction in the answer must be changed to the next cent.

Sample Solution

$$\frac{.08+}{12)\ 1.00} \text{ equals } \$.09 \text{ a can, or } 9¢ \text{ (not } .09¢)$$

Notes

Units	Weight
12 items equal 1 dozen	2,000 pounds equals 1 ton
144 items equal 1 gross	16 ounces equal 1 pound

Distance	Liquids
12 inches equal 1 foot	4 quarts equal 1 gallon
3 feet equal 1 yard	2 pints equal 1 quart
1,760 yards equal 1 mile	4 glasses equal 1 quart
5,280 feet equal 1 mile	1 glass equals 8 ounces

Notice that ounces may be used to measure liquids (an 8 ounce glass) or weight (8 ounces or 1/2 pound of butter). There are 16 ounces in a pound, but 32 ounces in a quart.

Problems

Units

1. Find the cost of 1 bottle of soda at $1.50 per dozen.

2. Find the cost of 1 bottle of soda at $.85 per dozen.

3. Find the cost of 1 bottle of soda at $1.10 per dozen.

4. Find the cost of 1 bottle of soda at $1.75 per dozen.

5. What would 1 egg cost if eggs sell for $.73 per dozen?

6. What would 1 egg cost if eggs sell for $.62 per dozen?

7. If oranges cost $.96 per dozen, how much would 5 cost?

8. If lemons cost $.72 per dozen, how much would 4 cost?

Weight

9. Find the cost of 1/4 pound butter at $.85 per pound.

10. Find the cost of 1/2 pound butter at $.97 per pound.

11. What would 4 ounces of ham cost at $1.60 a pound?

12. What would 8 ounces of cheese cost at $1.10 a pound?

13. I have 128 ounces of sugar. How many one pound sacks will it fill?

14. How many one pound bags will be filled by 208 ounces of rice?

15. A car weighs 2½ tons. How many pounds does it weigh?

16. A truck weighs 4 tons. How many pounds does it weigh?

17. If ham sells for $1.79 a pound, what would one ounce cost?

18. What would two ounces of ham cost if it sells for $1.45 a pound?

19. An 8-ounce jar of coffee costs $1.04. What would one pound of coffee cost?

20. A 4-ounce jar of jam costs $.39. Find the cost of a pound of jam.

21. A box of soap powder costs $.34 and weighs 2 pounds 3 ounces. Another box of similar soap powder costs $.34 and weighs 34 ounces. Which is the better buy?

22. A bag of potato chips costs $.63 and weighs 1/2 pound. A similar box of potato chips costs $.63 and weighs 7 ounces. Which is the better buy?

Liquids

23. Find the cost of 1 pint of cream at $1.65 a quart.

24. Find the cost of 1 pint of cream at $1.43 a quart.

25. If I drink 2 glasses of milk each day, how many quarts have I drunk after 30 days?

26. If each guest at a party will drink one glass of soda, how many quart bottles should be bought for 24 guests? For 25 guests?

27. An 8-ounce bottle of soda costs $.09. A quart bottle of the same soda costs $.33. If I wanted a quart, how much would I save by buying the large bottle?

28. An 8-ounce bottle of soda costs $.07. If I wanted a quart, how much would I save by buying a quart bottle for $.25?

29. Your mother bought 4 quart jars of apple juice at $.29 a quart. How much would she have saved by buying a gallon jar for $.98?

30. John drank a 6 ounce bottle of coke daily. How many quarts did he drink after 32 days?

Distance

31. A runner ran a mile and one half. How many feet did he run?

32. A desk is 60 inches long. How many feet long is it?

33. A roll of Scotch tape 7 feet long, costs $.42. A roll of the same brand 36 inches long costs $.21. Which is the better buy?

34. A room is 6 yards long. What is the length in feet?

SECTION 4   Retail Invoices

Class Drill

Add:	Add:	Add:	Add:
1. $75	2. $821	3. $6.42	4. $8.50
86	643	9.75	.35
94	272	2.19	6.48
37		.45	1.20

Sample Problem

Sara Jenkins of 342 State St., N.Y.C. bought these articles at Simpson's Department Store, 25 Fourth Avenue, N.Y.C.

3 white shirts at $3.95
2 ties   at   2.25

Prepare the sales slip.

Explanation

The New York City sales tax rate is 7%.
On amounts under $1.00 a special tax chart should be used, as shown below.
On amounts over $1.00 the 7% rate should be used.

Amount of Sale	Tax
$.01 to $.10	None
.11 to .20	1¢
.21 to .33	2¢
.34 to .47	3¢
.48 to .62	4¢
.63 to .76	5¢
.77 to .91	6¢
.92 to 1.07	7¢

Sample Solution

SIMPSON'S DEPARTMENT STORE
25 FOURTH AVENUE
NEW YORK, N.Y. 10003

Sept. 10   19___

SOLD TO Sara Jenkins

Address 342 State St. N.Y.C.

CLERK	DEPT.	AMT. REC'D.

QUAN.	DESCRIPTION	AMOUNT	
3	white shirts @ 3.95	11	85
2	ties @ 2.25	4	50
		16	35
	Sales tax	1	14
		17	49

POSITIVELY NO EXCHANGES MADE UNLESS
THIS SLIP IS PRESENTED WITHIN 3 DAYS.

Tax Computation
16.35
×.07
1.1445 = $1.14 Sales Tax

7

The tax is imposed on sales of merchandise sold at retail in New York City; on restaurant meals (effective 7/1/71); on hotel rentals; on night club charges; on admissions to places of amusement (except movies, dramatic or musical arts performances or events which are subject to another state tax); on certain services, such as repair charges, storage charges. The buyer must pay the tax.

Some retail sales are not taxed: sales of food (but candy is taxed); sales of beverages (but soft drinks, beer and other alcoholic beverages are taxed); sales of drugs and medicines (but cosmetics and toiletries are taxed); sales of eyeglasses; sales of newspapers and periodicals; sales of goods purchased for resale; sales of goods delivered outside of New York State for use outside of New York State.

The *compensating use tax* is imposed on merchandise purchased outside of New York State but used inside of New York State. The rate of tax is the same as the sales tax.

Sales made in New York City for delivery to places outside of New York City, but within New York State, are subject to the New York State sales tax of 4%.

Notes

1. To multiply by a per cent, first change the per cent to a decimal. "Per cent" means "by the hundred," therefore to change a per cent to a decimal, move the decimal point two places to the left and drop the per cent sign.

   Examples: 7% = .07
   8.5% = .085

2. If the answer has more than two decimal places, find the answer to the nearest cent. To do this, look at the third decimal place. If it is a five or higher, change the answer to the next cent; if it is a four or lower, drop the remaining decimals.

   Examples: $2.5263 = $2.53
   $1.2348 = $1.23

Problems

1. Find the New York City sales tax on each of these sales:

a. $10	f. $.30	k. $1.07	p. $12.10	u. $73.01
b. $35	g. $.70	l. $1.20	q. $48.67	v. $29.99
c. $18	h. $.50	m. $2.55	r. $39.28	w. $19.99
d. $120	i. $.05	n. $4.90	s. $145.50	x. $23.98
e. $84	j. $.95	o. $3.15	t. $178.15	y. $10.10

2. Prepare the sales slip for the following sale made today to H. Dale, 1450 31 Ave., Long Island City. The store is B. Bentley & Co., 123 Steinway St., Long Island City.

   4 white shirts at $3.25
   7 pairs socks at $1.25

8

3. Prepare the sales slip for this sale made today at Wayne's Department Store, 85 Broadway, New York City, to Mrs. Tom Donovan, 1815 4th Ave., N.Y.C.

> 7 pairs hose   at $ 1.59
> 2 pairs slacks at $14.75

4. You are working at the A.B.C. Co., 55 Worth St., New York City, as a sales clerk. Write the sales slips for the following sales you made today.
   a. Sale made to Mrs. John Hayes, 1010 Broadway, New York City

   > 2 pairs stockings at $1.35
   > 3 aprons at $.85
   > 1 slip at $2.98

   b. Sale made to Miss F. Hanley, 3200 Flatbush Ave., Brooklyn, New York

   > 1/2 dozen glasses at $4.50 per dozen
   > 4 yards fabric at $1.35 a yard
   > 6 plates at $24 a dozen

5. The following sales were made in a New York City supermarket. What sales tax would be added to the bill in each case, and what total would have to be paid by each customer? (*Note:* To find the tax, first separate the taxable items, get a total of these items, and find the tax. Add the tax to the total of all the items.)

a. Lamb chops	$2.40		b. Cleaning fluid	$ .42
Paper towels	.38		Coca Cola	.75
Apples	.49		Orange juice	.60
Soap	.29		Lettuce	.29
c. Bread	.31		d. Ginger ale	.59
Flour	.43		Wax paper	.33
Beer	1.25		Chicken	2.50
Onions	.35		Stringbeans	.43
e. Butter	.79		f. Candy	1.35
Paper napkins	.33		Shaving cream	.57
Soap	.42		Magazine	.20
Envelopes	.25		Meat	2.30

6. Mr. Jones, who lives in the Bronx, bought a new car outside of New York State for $3,400. If he uses the car in New York City, how much compensating use tax will he have to pay?

7. Miss Town bought a new car outside of N.Y. State for $2,950. She returned to her home in New York City. How much compensating use tax will she have to pay?

9

8. Mr. Brenner bought a new car in New York City for $3,650, and was allowed $825 on the trade-in of his old car. How much sales tax must he pay? (*Note:* The value of the trade-in may be deducted from the price in order to find the sales tax.)

9. Mr. Tompkins bought a car in New York City for $2,975. If he traded in his old car and was allowed $150, what did he pay for his new car, including the sales tax?

10. Mrs. Smith, who lives in New Jersey, bought several dresses and a coat in a New York City store. She told the seller to deliver the merchandise to her home. How much sales tax must she pay, if the total bill was $225?

SECTION 5 — Retail Discounts

Class Drill

Add:	Add:	
1. $17.50	2. $ 1.24	3. Find 7% of $15 6. Find 10% of $75
33.45	21.57	4. Find 7% of $135 7. Multiply 75 by 10
6.22	3.45	5. Find 10% of $80 8. Multiply 8.6 by 10
8.47	9.17	

Sample Problem

In a special sale the ABC Department Store marked down men's slacks by 10%. What would be the selling price on slacks marked to sell, before the sale, for $15?

Explanation

From time to time stores offer discounts to customers for various reasons: to sell merchandise near the end of a season, to sell merchandise that has been in the store for a long time, to attract customers, etc. The discount, or markdown, is merely a method used to reduce the marked price of goods.

Sample Solution

$15 Marked Price
×.10
1.50 Retail Discount

$15.00 Marked Price
1.50 Retail Discount
13.50 Selling Price

Notes

10% = .10 = 1/10. When we take 10% of a number, we are dividing by 10. Remember the shortcut: to divide by 10, move the decimal point one place to the left.

Problems

1. During a sale, an item that originally sold for $25 was marked down 10%. What was the new selling price?

2. Brown's Department Store advertised a 10% discount on a certain dress marked to sell for $14. What would the dress sell for after taking the retail discount?

10

3. A toy store marked down all merchandise 10% after January 1. If toys are marked as follows, how much would a customer pay for each after the store deducted the discount?

   a. $2.00   c. $8.25   e. $14.50   g. $17.35
   b. $4.50   d. $3.45   f. $ 1.20   h. $ .90

4. Find the selling price of the following items after markdown.

	Marked Price	Retail Discount
a.	$16.00	10%
b.	$24.00	15%
c.	$35.00	20%
d.	$70.00	15%
e.	$ 6.50	10%
f.	$12.90	10%
g.	$17.50	15%
h.	$24.40	20%

5. An employee of McGee's Department Store in New York City may buy at a discount of 20%. Find the cost of the following purchases made by an employee before the sales tax, and then after the sales tax has been added. (Note: The sales tax is taken on the actual selling price, not on the marked price.)

   a. $5.00   e. $8.00
   b. $25.00   f. $9.50
   c. $40.00   g. $24.00
   d. $35.00   h. $16.00

SECTION 6   Wholesale Invoices: Trade Discounts

Class Drill

1. Find 10% of $175

2. Find 25% of $480

3. Find 50% of $86

4. Find 40% of $25

5. Divide $870 by 10

6. Divide $32 by 10

7. Divide $430 by 10

8. Divide $6.25 by 10

Sample Problems

1. A wholesaler sold a radio listed at $60 in the catalog, subject to a trade discount of 40%. Find the price to the retailer.

2. A manufacturer sold a TV set listed at $400 in his catalog subject to trade discounts of 25% and 10%. Find the selling price.

Explanation

Manufacturers and wholesalers issue catalogs to show their merchandise and prices to be charged to the consumer. When they sell merchandise to retailers in the trade, they allow one or more trade discounts, shown on dis-

count sheets, so that the retailer pays less than the price shown in the catalog. If there is a single discount, it is deducted from the list price to find the selling price, in a manner similar to retail discounts, as explained on page 10. If there is more than one discount, the second discount is found by applying the per cent to the amount left after deducting the first discount; the third discount is found by applying the per cent to the amount left after deducting the second discount.

Sample Solutions

Problem 1.

$60 List Price
× .40
―――――――――
$24.00 Trade Discount

$60.00 List Price
24.00 Trade Discount
―――――――――
$36.00 Selling Price

Problem 2

$400 List Price
Less 25% 100 First Discount
―――――――――
$300
Less 10%   30 Second Discount
―――――――――
$270 Selling Price

Use these short cuts:
  To find 10% of a number, move the decimal point one place to the left.
  To find 25% of a number, take 1/4 of the number.
  To find 50% of a number, take 1/2 of the number.

Problems

1. Find the cost of a radio listed at $50, less a trade discount of 10%.

2. Find the cost of each item after deducting the trade discount:
   a. $175 less 20%
   b. $340 less 10%
   c. $162 less 10%
   d. $248.55 less 10%
   e. $462 less 50%
   f. $164 less 25%
   g. $244 less 25%.
   h. $74 less 50%
   i. $75 less 20%
   j. $65 less 40%
   k. $190.50 less 10%
   l. $1.98 less 10%

3. a. A washing machine sells for $240 less trade discounts of 25% and 10%. Find the selling price.
   b. If the washing machine sold for $240 less trade discounts of 10% and 25%, would the answer be the same? Why?

4. a. A TV set listed at $500 is sold subject to trade discounts of 20% and 10%. Find the selling price.
   b. If the TV set were sold less a trade discount of 30% (20% plus 10%), would the answer be the same? Why?

5. Find the selling price in each of the following:
   a. $150 less 20% and 10%
   b. $40 less 25% and 10%
   c. $150 less 50% and 10%
   d. $120 less 25% and 20%
   e. $130 less 20% and 10%
   f. $50 less 25% and 10%
   g. $200 less 25%, 20% and 10%
   h. $175 less 20%, 10% and 5%

6. A radio sells for $175 less 20% and 10%.
   a. Find the selling price.
   b. If another radio sells for $175 less 30%, would it cost more or less?
   c. Why aren't the answers to (a) and (b) the same?

7. A refrigerator, marked to sell for $160, is sold to the retailer with discounts of 40% and 10%.
   a. Find the price to the retailer.
   b. If the retailer obtained discounts of 10% and 40%, how much would he pay?
   c. Look at your two answers. How do they compare? What conclusion can you draw?

8. A lamp sells for $40, less discounts of 20% and 5%.
   a. Find the cost.
   b. What would the cost be if the discount had been 25%.
   c. What would the cost be if the discounts were 15% and 10%.
   d. Suppose the discounts were 5% and 20%. Find the cost.
   e. Compare your answers. What conclusions can you draw?

SECTION 7 Wholesale Invoices: Finding a Single Trade Discount

Class Drill

1. Divide 670 by 100
2. Divide 35 by 10
3. Divide 72.4 by 10
4. Divide 61.1 by 100
5. Find 10% of $17.00
6. Find 25% of $36.40
7. Find 10% of $85.50
8. Find 50% of $142.24

Sample Problem   What single trade discount would equal 20% and 10%?

Explanation   If the same discount series of two or more discounts must be used for many items, conversion to a single discount will save time in finding selling prices.

Sample Solution

```
              100%  List Price
    Less 20%   20   First Discount
               80
    Less 10%    8   Second Discount
               72%  Selling Price                Check

              100%  List Price              20%  First Discount
               72   Selling Price            8%  Second Discount
               28%  Discount                28%  Single Discount
```

Problems
1. a. What single discount is the same as discounts of 25% and 20%?
   b. Why isn't the answer 45%?

13

2. Find the single discount equal to discounts of 20% and 20%.

3. In each case find the single discount equal to the two discounts:
   a. 40% and 10%   e. 50% and 10%
   b. 30% and 10%   f. 40% and 20%
   c. 10% and 10%   g. 25% and 5%
   d. 25% and 10%   h. 35% and 10%

4. A firm buys four articles from a manufacturer, all subject to trade discounts of 25% and 20%. The first article has a list price of $60, the second has a list price of $160, the third $200, the fourth $260.
   a. Use the trade discounts to find the cost of each item.
   b. What single discount would be equal to the two discounts?
   c. Use your answer to (b) to find the cost of each item.
   d. Are your answers to (a) and (c) the same?

5. A wholesaler buys merchandise at list price less 20% and 5%.
   a. If the wholesaler buys items for $50, $75, $125, and $150, find the cost of each item, after deducting the two trade discounts.
   b. What single discount equals the two discounts?
   c. Use the single discount to find the cost of each of the four items.
   d. Are your answers to (a) and (c) the same?

SECTION 8   Wholesale Invoices: Cash Discounts

Class Drill

1. Find 1% of $120   5. Find 3% of $75

2. Find 1% of $35   6. Find 3% of $145

3. Find 2% of $60   7. Find 2% of $80

4. Find 2% of $40   8. Find 1% of $61.25

Sample Problem

On March 14, goods were sold for $350, terms 2/10 n/30.
   a. By what date must payment be made to obtain the discount?
   b. How much is the cash discount?
   c. How much must the buyer pay if he is entitled to the discount?
   d. What is the last date for payment without the discount?

Explanation

Manufacturers and wholesalers wish to obtain payment for merchandise as quickly as possible. To encourage the buyer to pay quickly, cash discounts are offered. Terms 2/10 n/30 mean that the seller will allow the buyer to deduct a cash discount of 2% if he pays the bill within 10 days of the date of sale. If the buyer does not wish to pay quickly, he may take 30 days from the date of sale to pay the full amount.

Sample Solution

a. March 14 plus 10 days is March 24.

b. $350 Selling Price
   ×.02
   7.00 Cash Discount

c. $350 Selling Price
   ___7 Cash Discount
   $343 Cash Paid

d. March 14 plus 30 days : April 13
   March 14 to March 31 17 days
   April 1 to April 13   13 days
                          30 days

Notes

a. *Use this shortcut:*
   To take 1% of a number, move the decimal point two places to the left. (Same rule as dividing by 100)

b. *Remember:*
   30 days has September, April, June, November
   All the rest have 31, except February 28 (leap year 29)

c. *Shortcut:*
   30 days from any date in a month having 30 days is the same date in the following month. Ex.: April 4 plus 30 is May 4

d. *Shortcut:*
   30 days from any date in a month having 31 days is one day sooner in the following month. Ex.: July 8 plus 30 is August 7

Problems

1. A sale amounting to $150 was made subject to a cash discount of 2%.
   a. What was the cash discount?
   b. How much cash was paid after taking the discount?

2. In each problem, find (a) the cash discount; (b) the net price
   a. $230 less 2%   e. $45.50 less 2%
   b. $165 less 1%   f. $130.25 less 1%
   c. $24 less 3%   g. $6.45 less 2%
   d. $180 less 2%   h. $186.43 less 2%

3. On March 14 merchandise was sold for $225, terms 2/10 n/30.
   a. How much should be paid on March 24?
   b. How much should be paid on April 13?

4. What date would be 30 days from:
   a. June 10   d. November 8   g. February 8 (not leap year)
   b. September 6   e. April 30   h. December 31
   c. March 29   f. July 14   i. May 31

5. Goods were sold on April 16 for $260, terms 2/10 n/30.
   a. By what date should payment be made to obtain the cash discount?
   b. How much is the cash discount?
   c. How much must the buyer pay after deducting the discount?
   d. If the buyer does not want to pay early, by what date must he pay in full?

6-15. For each of the following problems answer the four questions shown in Problem 5.

	Date of Sale	Terms	Amount
6.	October 4	2/10 n/30	$200.00
7.	August 18	2/10 n/30	350.00
8.	April 25	2/10 n/30	123.00
9.	July 1	3/10 n/30	75.00
10.	September 13	3/10 n/60	360.00
11.	February 7	2/10 n/30	65.00
12.	December 19	2/10 n/60	125.00
13.	May 9	3/10 n/30	132.57
14.	July 7	2/10 n/30	249.63
15.	January 20	3/10 n/60	374.28

16. Mr. Johnson sells $400 worth of merchandise to Mr. Paul, terms 2/10 n/30. Mr. Paul tells Mr. Johnson that a 2% discount is not very much, because he can get 5% interest from a savings bank. Is this a good argument? How would you reply to Mr. Paul?

SECTION 9 Wholesale Invoices: Trade and Cash Discounts

Class Drill

1. Find 1% of $383.
2. Find 3% of $465.
3. Find 2% of $376.
4. Find 3% of $263.19

5. Find 10% of $435.
6. Find 10% of $149.25
7. Find 20% of $237.
8. Find 25% of $163.50

Sample Problem

On April 25, goods were sold to a retailer for $125 less 20%, terms 2/10 n/30.
  a. What was the selling price?
  b. How much should be paid on May 25?
  c. How much should be paid on May 5?

Explanation

The price to the retailer is not the list price of $125, because that is the price to the consumer. The selling price to the retailer is found by deducting the trade discount. If the retailer pays within 10 days, then he may deduct 2% from the selling price to find the amount of cash to be paid.

Sample Solution

a)
```
          $125 List Price
Less 20%    25 Trade Discount
          $100 Selling Price
```

b) Pay $100 on May 25

c)
```
$100 Selling Price   $100 Selling Price
 .02                   2 Discount
2.00 Cash Discount    98 Paid on May 5
```

Problems

1. On September 14 a retailer bought merchandise listed at $240, less 25%, terms 2/10 n/30.
   a. How much must he pay on October 14?
   b. How much must he pay on September 24?

16

2. On June 23 goods were sold to a retailer for $200 less 20%, terms 2/10 n/30.

    a. If the retailer does not wish to take the cash discount, how much must he pay? By what date?

    b. If the retailer wishes to take the cash discount, how much must he pay? By what date?

3–18. In each of the following problems find:

    a. the amount to be paid, and the final date, if the buyer does not take the cash discount.

    b. the amount to be paid, and the final date, if the buyer takes the cash discount.

	Date of Sale	Amount	Trade Discount	Terms
3.	October 10	$220	40%	2/10 n/30
4.	September 14	300	20%	2/10 n/30
5.	March 6	50	10%	2/10 n/30
6.	May 10	125	20%	3/10 n/30
7.	February 3	200	25%	3/10 n/60
8.	March 29	175	10%	2/10 n/30
9.	November 5	145	20%	2/10 n/30
10.	May 24	152	10%	2/10 n/30
11.	October 4	240	25%	3/10 n/60
12.	March 8	350	20%	2/10 n/30
13.	September 10	300	20% and 10%	2/10 n/30
14.	January 3	800	25% and 10%	2/10 n/30
15.	July 18	250	20% and 10%	2/10 n/30
16.	December 15	450	20% and 10%	2/10 n/30
17.	November 24	120	25% and 10%	2/10 n/30
18.	January 21	180	25% and 10%	2/10 n/30

19. Goods were sold to a retailer on June 29, $250, less 20% and 5%, terms 2/10 n/30.

    a. How much should the retailer pay on July 9?

    b. How much should the retailer pay on July 29?

    c. If the retailer paid on July 20, how much should he pay?

20. On September 14 goods were sold to a retailer for $145 less 25% and 10%, terms 3/10 n/60.

    a. How much should be paid on September 24?

    b. How much should be paid on November 13?

SECTION 10   Invoicing Skills: Invoicing Review

Part I   Short Cuts

Solve each of the following problems using the short cuts you have learned. Do not use scrap paper. These problems should be done in your head.

1. Divide 650 by 10

2. Divide 32.4 by 10

3. Multiply 75 by 100

4. Multiply 43.7 by 100

5. Find 10% of $43.00

6. Find 10% of $7.58

7. Find 50% of $24

8. Find 50% of $1.20

9. Find 1% of $80

10. Find 1% of $35.80

11. Find 25% of $32

12. Find 25% of $8.24

13. Multiply 2.6 by 10

14. Find 10% of $14.30

15. Find 1% of $16.75

16. Find 50% of $27

17. Find 25% of $48.20

18. Multiply 3.54 by 1000

19. Divide 3.7 by 100

20. Divide 268 by 1000

Part II Problems

Solve each of the following problems in good form. Show all work on your answer paper. Do not use scrap paper.

1. Find the cost of 2,500 letterheads at $5 per C.

2. Find the cost of 6,400 envelopes at $14 per M.

3. What would 1 can of ginger ale cost if it sells at $1.10 per dozen?

4. Prepare the sales slip for a sale to George Billings, 1420 State St., New York City. The store is Green's Men's Shop, 48 Steinway St., Long Island City, N.Y. The sale was: 4 pairs hose at $1.30
   3 ties at $2.75

5. You have rung the following items on a cash register in a New York City store. What would the sales tax be for each customer? What would each customer have to pay?

a.		b.		c.	
Bread	$.31	Apple juice	$.41	Chicken	$2.43
Steak	2.46	Light bulb	.29	Shaving cream	.57
Ginger ale	.49	Butter	.79	Oranges	.62
Beer	1.05	Paper towels	.43	Candy	.75
Soap	.29	Paper napkins	.34	Sponges	.47

6. Bill Sullivan bought a new car in Newark, New Jersey and drove it back to his home in Queens. If the cost of the car was $3,150, how much compensating use tax would Bill have to pay New York City?

7. What would a radio cost the retailer if the list price is $85 and he is allowed trade discounts of 20% and 10%?

8. What single discount would equal discounts of 20% and 20%?

9. The ABC Co. sold goods on March 17 for $235 terms 2/10 n/30.
   a. In order to obtain the cash discount, by what date should the bill be paid?
   b. How much would the discount be?
   c. By what date must the entire bill be paid if no discount is desired?

10. The Miller Manufacturing Co. sold $375 worth of goods on July 20, subject to a trade discount of 20%, terms 3/10 n/60.
    a. If the buyer did not wish to take the cash discount, by what date would he have to pay the bill?
    b. How much would he have to pay on the above date?
    c. If he paid the bill on July 28, how much would he have to pay?

UNIT 2

Paying by Check

SECTION 1 — Preparing the Bank Deposit

Class Drill

Multiply:

1. 14 × .10	6. 40 × .25	11. 18 × .50	16. 34 × .01	21. 17 × .10
2. 18 × .10	7. 48 × .25	12. 22 × .50	17. 79 × .01	22. 64 × .25
3. 110 × .10	8. 60 × .25	13. 6 × .50	18. 123 × .01	23. 46 × .50
4. 34 × .10	9. 18 × .25	14. 13 × .50	19. 240 × .01	24. 109 × .01
5. 139 × .10	10. 14 × .25	15. 17 × .50	20. 135 × .01	25. 35 × .10

Sample Problem

Mr. Briggs owns a small retail store. He made the following deposit in the First National Bank on April 4: 7 ten-dollar bills, 18 one-dollar bills, 22 half-dollars, 48 quarters, 32 dimes, 6 nickels, 249 pennies, and checks for $25.00 and $10.00

a. Prepare the deposit slip.

b. If the cash register tape showed total sales of $151.99, was the amount of the deposit correct?

Explanation

In order to prepare the deposit slip, Mr. Briggs first prepares a tally slip to find how much cash he has on hand. He then prepares the deposit slip, listing cash first, and then each check separately. By looking at the cash register tape he can tell how much the sales were for the day. The amount of the deposit should agree with the tape. If he started the day with a change fund in the cash register, the bills and coins of the change fund should be put back into the register before making the deposit.

Notes

> The shortcuts you learned previously should be used in these problems:
> 10% equals .10, hence to multiply move the decimal point one place to left.
> 50% equals .50, hence to multiply take 1/2.
> 25% equals .25, hence to multiply take 1/4.
> 1% equals .01, hence to multiply move the decimal point two places to left.

19

Sample Solution

CASH TALLY SHEET		
DATE _April 4_		
BILLS	NUMBER	AMOUNT
$20		
$10	7	70 00
$ 5		
$ 1	18	18 00
COINS		
.50	22	11 00
.25	48	12 00
.10	32	3 20
.05	6	30
.01	249	2 49
TOTAL		116 99

Deposited with Bank

Date _April 4_   19

Please use your PERSONALIZED DEPOSIT TICKETS.
To order more, use your reorder card or ask a teller.

For Account of (Please print full name and account number)

JOHN BRIGGS
714 STEINWAY ST.
LONG ISLAND CITY, N.Y.

Account Number 9 8 7 — 6 5 4 3 2 1

BANK   Checking Account Deposit

Bank Use Only

Chk.

Less Dep.

Ret'd

Units

	Dollars	Cents
Cash Include Coupons	116	99
Checks List Separately 1	25	00
2	10	00
3		
4		
5		
6		
7		
8		
Total	151	99

The cash register tape, $151.99, agrees with the deposit slip.

Problems

1. Your father deposited the following bills and coins in his account in the Chemical New York Trust Co. on January 7: 4 ten-dollar bills, 2 five-dollar bills, 8 one-dollar bills, 12 quarters, 16 dimes, 4 nickels, and 24 pennies. He also deposited a check for $12.50 and a check for $14.00.
   a. Prepare the cash tally to show the total cash he deposited.
   b. Prepare the deposit slip.

2. On July 8 Henry Thompson, owner of a small store, made the following deposit in the First National Bank:
   - 16 ten-dollar bills
   - 9 five-dollar bills
   - 34 one-dollar bills
   - 6 half-dollars
   - 27 quarters
   - 51 dimes
   - 14 nickels
   - 106 pennies
     checks for $17.50 and $33.20.

a. Prepare the cash tally to show the total cash deposit.

b. Prepare the deposit slip.

3. George Daniels deposited the following in the Chase Manhattan Bank each day during the week:

	May 18	May 19	May 20	May 21	May 22
$20 bills	7	8	4	15	—
$10 bills	19	21	37	43	58
$5 bills	8	11	15	12	15
$1 bills	73	104	61	75	65
Half dollars	5	16	23	—	—
Quarters	16	29	41	52	43
Dimes	32	41	56	38	59
Nickels	14	20	24	—	18
Pennies	65	108	223	119	256
Checks for	$12.00	$17.40	$29.30	$33.60	$19.25
Checks for	$18.00	$32.70	$23.60	—	$17.40
Checks for	$21.00	$14.18	$14.85	—	—

a. Prepare the cash tally each day.

b. Prepare the deposit slip each day.

c. If Mr. Daniels started each day with an empty cash register, what total should the tape in the cash register show each day?

4. On September 6 William Harris deposited 4 ten-dollar bills, 17 one-dollar bills, 46 quarters, 28 dimes, 106 pennies.

a. Prepare the cash tally.

b. The cash register tape showed total sales of $72.36. Was the amount of cash correct?

5. The Tastee Bake Shop starts each day with a change fund of $25.00. At the end of the day the following bills and coins were in the register: 6 ten-dollar bills, 23 one-dollar bills, 25 quarters, 18 dimes and 76 pennies.

a. How much money was in the cash register at the end of the day?

b. The tape in the register showed total sales were $66.81. Was the amount of cash in the register correct?

6. Business firms usually wrap coins before taking them to the bank for deposit. How much would each of the following packages be worth?

Roll of 50 pennies

Roll of 40 nickels

Roll of 50 dimes

Roll of 40 quarters

Roll of 20 half-dollars

SECTION 2   Keeping the Checkbook

Class Drill

1. Add down, then check your answer by adding up:

a. $234.18	b. $359.17	c. $12.88	d. $29.64	e. $47.75
75.78	42.19	176.79	37.19	31.23
22.19	81.23	32.85	85.28	72.48

2. Subtract, then check your answers by adding remainders to subtrahends:

a. $429.17	b. $1,259.84	c. $2,495.16	d. $250.00	e. $2,595.00
132.19	276.15	143.23	12.11	175.16

Sample Problem

Mr. Briggs wishes to pay his April telephone bill, $13.45, on May 5. Prepare the check. (His bank is the First National Bank)

Explanation

When Mr. Briggs opened his checking account, he deposited money in the bank, was asked to sign a signature card and was given a blank checkbook, consisting of 3 checks on a page. He wishes to pay bills by check for several reasons: the checkbook stub is a record of how he spent his money; the cancelled checks prove that he paid the bill; the checks may be used conveniently and provide greater safety than if he used cash. Mr. Briggs first writes the stub of the check, which is kept in the checkbook, and he then writes the check, which he mails to the telephone company.

Sample Solution

Notes

1. The balance may be obtained after each page of checks has been written, or after each check. Your teacher will tell you which method to use.

2. Deposits should be added to the balance, either on the back of the stubs or on the front. Your teacher will tell you which method to use.

3. If you make an error on a check, print "VOID" on the stub and the check, and start over again on the next stub.

To the Teacher

Give each student a checkbook of 3 pages of checks, 3 checks on a page. Six checks will be needed; the remaining three checks are in reserve if checks are voided.

Problem

George Harris, owner of a small store, had a balance in the Second National Bank of $750.00 on October 1.
   a. Enter the balance in his checkbook.
   b. Enter deposits in the checkbook.
   c. Write the stubs and checks. (After you have written the first page of checks your teacher may tell you to write stubs only.)
   d. Show the balance in the checkbook at the end of the month.

22

October 2 Sent check #150 to the New York Telephone Co. for September bill, $8.50.
"   4 Sent check to Goldstein Bros., $17.25, for envelopes and stationery.
"   5 Deposited $125.00
"   10 Gave a check for $80.00 to Albert Beam, an employee, for his salary for the week.
"   16 Sent a check for $68.42 to the Beacon Advertising Co. for advertising.
"   22 Deposited $85.25.
"   24 Cashed a check for $50.00
"   27 Paid the General Typewriter Repair Co. $23.79 to repair the typewriter.

SECTION 3 Finding the Checkbook Balance

Class Drill

1. Add down, then check your answer by adding up:

a. $129.17	b. $45.00	c. $122.00	d. $42.00	e. $45.30
42.19	135.00	43.00	17.85	18.00
33.00	78.60	1.25	4.95	65.00

2. Subtract, then check your answers by adding remainders to subtrahends:

a. $350.00	b. $475.20	c. $749.51	d. $786.00	e. $642.19
49.17	162.00	632.19	91.20	85.22

Sample Problem

Mr. George Harris (see previous problem regarding Mr. George Harris) has kept his checkbook for the month of October. Checks and deposits have been written on the stubs as follows:

First Page of Checks			*Second Page of Checks*		
Date	*No.*	*Amount*	*Date*	*No.*	*Amount*
Oct. 2	150	$8.50	Oct. 16	153	$68.42
4	151	17.25	24	154	50.00
10	152	80.00	27	155	23.79

First Page of Deposits
Oct. 4 $125.00

Second Page of Deposits
Oct. 22 $85.25

a. What was the checkbook balance on October 10?
b. What was the checkbook balance on October 31?

Explanation

Refer to your checkbook. It should show the same information as shown in the sample problem. If you had to void a check, you will have some checks on different pages, and you will have checks on the third page.

In some checkbooks, the balance is found after each page of checks has been completed. In other checkbooks the balance is found after writing each check. Your teacher will tell you which method to use.

Method 1
Finding the balance after each page
  a. *Checks on page 1*

$ 8.50	$750.00	Bal. Oct. 1
17.25	125.00	Deposit Oct. 5
80.00	875.00	
105.75	105.75	Total checks page 1
	769.25	Bal. Oct. 10

  b. *Checks on page 2*

$ 68.42	$769.25	Bal. Oct. 10
50.00	85.25	Deposit Oct. 22
23.79	854.50	
142.21	142.21	Total checks page 2
	712.29	Bal. Oct. 31

Method 2
Finding the balance after each check

a.		b.	
$750.00	Bal. Oct. 1	$769.25	Bal. Oct. 10
8.50	Check Oct. 2	68.42	Check Oct. 16
741.50	Bal. Oct. 2	700.83	Bal. Oct. 16
17.25	Check Oct. 4	85.25	Deposit Oct. 22
724.25	Bal. Oct. 4	786.08	Bal. Oct. 22
125.00	Deposit Oct. 5	50.00	Check Oct. 24
849.25	Bal. Oct. 5	736.08	Bal. Oct. 24
80.00	Check Oct. 10	23.79	Check Oct. 27
769.25	Bal. Oct. 10	712.29	Bal. Oct. 31

Problems

(*Note:* Problems 1, 2 and 3 have been arranged to find the balance after each page of checks. Problems 4 and 5 have been arranged to find the balance after each check.)

1. Peter Davis had a balance in his checkbook on June 1 of $800. His checkbook showed the following stubs and deposits during June:

First Page of Checks			Second Page of Checks		
Date	No.	Amount	Date	No.	Amount
June 2	101	$12.00	June 17	104	$15.50
5	102	75.00	23	105	21.20
12	103	60.00	28	106	10.75

First Page of Deposits	Second Page of Deposits
June 8 $100.00	June 25 $125.00

  a. What was the balance on June 12?
  b. What was the balance on June 30?

2. Henry Brennan had a balance in his checking account of $625 on April 1. His checkbook showed the following stubs and deposits during April:

First Page of Checks			Second Page of Checks			Third Page of Checks		
Date	No.	Amount	Date	No.	Amount	Date	No.	Amount
April 3	250	$ 4.15	April 11	253	$14.40	April 17	256	$19.95
6	251	17.62	13	254	26.32	23	257	16.40
10	252	12.75	14	255	15.95	26	258	32.00

First Page of Deposits	Second Page of Deposits	Third Page of Deposits
April 9 $75.00	April 12 $150.00	April 19 $50.00
		24 25.00

a. What was the balance on April 10?
b. What was the balance on April 15?
c. What was the balance on April 30?

3. William Haddad's checkbook showed a March 1 balance of $640. During March the following checks were written and deposits made.

First Page of Checks			Second Page of Checks			Third Page of Checks		
March 2	#75	$12.45	March 8	#78	$ 1.23	March 15	#81	$35.00
3	#76	6.87	10	#79	16.38	18	#82	27.95
5	#77	18.59	12	#80	22.19	19	#83	14.33

First Page of Deposits	Second Page of Deposits	Third Page of Deposits
March 4 $25.00	March 10 $100.00	March 16 $23.00
	11 50.00	19 45.00

a. What was the balance on March 6?
b. What was the balance on March 13?
c. What was the balance on March 31?

4. Norman Peter's checkbook showed the following entries during the month of September:

September	1	Balance	$500.00
	2	Check #40	14.55
	4	Check #41	18.25
	6	Deposit	100.00
	9	Check #42	6.41
	14	Check #43	17.58
	15	Deposit	75.00
	18	Check #44	31.50
	22	Check #45	23.40

a. What was the balance on September 10?
b. What was the balance on September 30?

5. Norman Peter's checkbook (see problem 4) showed these entries the next month:

$$
\begin{array}{llll}
\text{October} & 5 & \text{Check \#46} & \$13.75 \\
& 7 & \text{Check \#47} & 22.40 \\
& 8 & \text{Check \#48} & 9.28 \\
& 10 & \text{Deposit} & 75.00 \\
& 12 & \text{Check \#49} & 18.42 \\
& 20 & \text{Check \#50} & 41.20 \\
\end{array}
$$

a. What was the balance on October 8? REMEMBER TO START WITH THE BALANCE ON Oct. 1.

b. What was the balance on October 31?

SECTION 4   Reconciling the Checkbook Balance with the Bank Balance

Class Drill

Add down; check by adding up. Use combination of 10 when possible.

1. $75.40	2. $172.19	3. $43.92	4. $24.77	5. $26.44
24.32	35.91	17.18	16.33	19.76
17.58	15.52	41.19	21.18	20.34

Sample Problem

On November 2 George Harris (see sample problem, page 23) received the following statement from his bank.

SECOND NATIONAL BANK

Mr. George Harris
2515 State St.
New York, N. Y.

ACCOUNT NO. **723 304322**
Closing Date: Oct. 31, 19 ——

Date Forwarded	Oct. 1, 19 ——	Balance Forwarded	750.00

Date	Checks	Deposits	Balance
Oct. 5	8.50	125.00	866.50
12	80.00		786.50
22	17.25	85.25	854.50
24	50.00		804.50

Enclosed with this bank statement Mr. Harris found the following checks:

$$
\begin{array}{lll}
\text{Check \#150} & \$ & 8.50 \\
\#152 & & 80.00 \\
\#151 & & 17.25 \\
\#154 & & 50.00 \\
\end{array}
$$

Explain why the closing balance shown in the bank statement does not agree with the closing balance shown in the checkbook. Show that the checkbook balance and the bank statement balance are both correct.

Explanation

The checkbook balance will not agree with the balance shown on the bank statement in any of the following situations:

1. The bank does not know of some checks written during the month. This would occur if a person who received a check did not cash it or deposit it, but kept it. Such a check is called an "OUTSTANDING CHECK".

2. The bank charged Mr. Harris a service charge, but he did not know of this charge until he received the bank statement.

3. Mr. Harris deposited some money near the end of the month, but the bank did not record it on the bank statement. This is called a "DEPOSIT IN TRANSIT".

4. An error made by the bank or by Mr. Harris.

Mr. Harris must decide which of the above possibilities caused the balance shown in the bank statement to be different from the balance shown in his checkbook. If he can "reconcile" these balances, that is, bring them together, then he knows no error was made.

Sample Solution

George Harris
Bank Reconciliation Statement
October 31, 19—

Checkbook Balance	$712.29	Bank Statement Balance	$804.50
		Less, Outstanding Checks:	
		# 153	68.42
		# 155	23.79
		Total Outstanding Checks	82.21
Corrected Balance	$712.29	Corrected Balance	$712.29

Problems

1. On May 2, Henry Brennan (see problem 2, page 25) received his bank statement showing a balance on April 30 of $828.26. Included with the statement were these cancelled checks: #250, $4.15; #251, $17.62; #252, $12.75; #254, $26.32; #255, $15.95; #256, $19.95.
   a. Which checks were outstanding on April 30?
   b. Reconcile the balance shown in the bank statement with the balance of $765.46 shown in the checkbook on April 30.

2. On April 3 William Haddad (see problem 3, page 25) received his bank statement showing a balance on March 31 of $758.72. Mr. Haddad found the following cancelled checks with the bank statement: #75, #76, #77, #78, #80, #81, #82.
   a. Which checks were outstanding on March 31?
   b. Reconcile the balance shown on the bank statement with the balance of $728.01 shown in the checkbook on March 31.

3. Norman Peters (see problem 4, page 25) received his bank statement on October 2, showing a September 30 balance of $624.62, and also the following cancelled checks: #40, #41, #43.
   a. Which checks were outstanding on September 30?
   b. Reconcile the balance shown on the bank statement with the balance of $563.31 in the checkbook on September 30.

4. Norman Peters, (see previous problem and problem 5 on page 26) received his bank statement on November 3, showing a balance on October 31 of $583.74 and also the following cancelled checks: #42, #44, #45, #46, #47, #49.
   a. Which checks were outstanding on October 31? (REMEMBER TO LOOK AT THE RECONCILIATION STATEMENT you prepared on September 30 for problem 3).
   b. Reconcile the balance shown in the bank statement on October 31 with the balance of $533.26 in the checkbook on October 31.

5. Elmer Town's checkbook showed a balance on June 30 of $975.00. His bank statement showed a balance on June 30 of $1000.00. When Mr. Town arranged his cancelled checks in order and compared them with the stubs in his checkbook, he found that two checks were not returned by the bank: #85, $15.00; and #87, $10.00. Reconcile the checkbook balance and his bank statement balance.

6. Barry Denver's checkbook showed a balance of $1,258.25 on April 30. His bank statement showed a balance of $1,287.75 on April 30. After looking at the cancelled checks, he found that #72 for $14.00 and #73 for $17.50 were not returned by the bank. He also found a slip from the bank, showing a bank charge of $2.00 for the month. Reconcile the checkbook balance and the bank statement balance.

7. George Steven's checkbook balance was $2,357.60 on June 30. His bank statement showed a balance of $2,517.35 on June 30. Mr. Stevens compared his cancelled checks with the checkbook stubs and found that these checks were not paid by the bank: #174, $120.00; #176, $43.25. Enclosed with the statement was a service charge of $3.50 made by the bank. Reconcile the checkbook balance and the bank statement balance.

8. Arthur Levin's checkbook balance on September 30 was $972.15. His bank statement showed a balance of $919.90 on September 30. The following checks were not returned by the bank: #271, $15.75, #272, $85.00. Looking at the bank statement, Mr. Levin noticed that a deposit he had made on September 30 for $150.00 was not shown by the bank. He saw a bank charge of $3.00. Reconcile the checkbook balance and the balance on the bank statement.

9. Henry Stein's checkbook showed a balance of $1,274.18 on November 30. His bank statement showed a balance on November 30 of $1,110.33. These checks were not cancelled by the bank: #125, $35.00; #128, $26.15. A deposit of $225.00 made on the evening of November 30 was not included in the bank statement. Reconcile the checkbook balance and the bank statement balance.

10. On March 15, David Madigan received his monthly bank statement showing a balance on March 10 of $2,375.44. Enclosed with the statement were the cancelled checks, but these checks were not included: #85, $31.00; #86, $12.75; and #87, which had been certified by Mr. Madigan, $150.00. There was a charge slip showing a bank charge of $2.25.
   a. Does a certified check which was not cashed, cause a difference between the balance shown in the bank statement and the balance shown in the checkbook? Explain.
   b. Prepare the reconciliation statement, if the checkbook balance on March 10 was $2,333.94.

11. On January 20, James Carter's checkbook balance was $1,328.00. His bank statement showed a balance on January 20 of $1,183.25. These checks were not returned by the bank: #148, $25.00; #149, which had been certified, $200.00; #150, $8.25. There was a bank charge of $3.00. A deposit, made late on January 19 for $175.00, was not shown on the bank statement. Reconcile the balance shown in the checkbook with the balance shown on the bank statement.

SECTION 5   Review Problems

1. On June 2, Henry Benton, owner of a retail store, made the following deposit in the Second National Bank:

> 4 twenty-dollar bills
> 13 ten-dollar bills
> 29 one-dollar bills
> 3 half-dollar coins
> 46 quarters
> 65 dimes
> 19 nickels
> 138 pennies
> checks for $8.50 and $14.95.

a. Prepare the cash tally to show the total cash deposited. (Either obtain a form from your teacher or make one similar to the one shown on page 20.)

b. Prepare the deposit slip. (Ask your teacher for a blank form.)

2. Assume you have your own checkbook. You wish to pay the Fancy Bike Store for a new bicycle you bought for $55.00. Using today's date, write the stub and check. (Your teacher will give you a blank form. If he has none, copy the form shown on page 22.)

3. Harold Smith's checkbook shows the following entries for September:

September	1	Balance	$653.00
	3	Check #25	35.20
	5	Deposit	54.00
	9	Check #26	17.25
	12	Check #27	9.17
	14	Deposit	45.00
	18	Check #28	20.00
	24	Check #29	1.55
	27	Deposit	130.00
	30	Check #30	50.75

a. If you have been taught to find the balance after each check, do so.

b. If you have been taught to find the balance after finishing a page of 3 checks, do so.

4. Barry Stern's checkbook balance on May 31 was $786.25. His bank statement showed a balance on May 31 of $854.10. When he compared his cancelled checks with the checkbook stubs, he found these checks were not included in the envelope: #75, $34.60; #77, $16.35; #78, $18.90. Included in the bank statement was a service charge of $2.00. Reconcile the checkbook balance and the bank statement balance.

UNIT 3

Interest

SECTION 1 **Interest Review**

Class Drill

1. Find 5% of $150
2. Find 5% of   78
3. Find 5% of   146.35
4. Find 4% of   241.25
5. Find 4% of   185.56

6. Find 6% of $150
7. Find 6% of   175
8. Find 6% of   146
9. Find 6% of   84.25
10. Find 6% of   163.48

Sample Problem   Mr. Ordway borrowed $250 from a friend for one-half year at 6% interest. How much will he have to repay?

Explanation   Interest rates are expressed as rates for one year, or "per annum." A 6% rate means that Mr. Ordway will have to pay 6% for each year that he borrows the money. To find the interest for one year, multiply the principal, which is the amount of the loan, by the rate expressed as a decimal, or .06. To find the interest for more than one year, first find the interest for one year, then multiply by the number of years. To find the interest for a fractional part of the year, first find the interest for one year, then multiply by the fraction.

Sample Solution

$250 Principal
× .06
$15.00 Interest for one year
½ × $15 = $7.50 Interest for ½ year

$250.00 Loan
7.50 Interest
$257.50 Repay

Problems

1. Find the interest for one year on each of the following amounts:
   a. $350 at 6%
   b. 430 at 5%
   c. 370 at 6%
   d. $152.20 at 6%
   e. 137.50 at 6%
   f. 149.23 at 5%

2. Find the interest in each of the following problems:
   a. $260 at 5% for 2 years
   b. 135 at 6% for 2 years
   c. $124 at 5% for 2 years
   d. 243 at 6% for 3 years

3. Find the interest:
   a. $200 at 5% for $\frac{1}{2}$ year
   b. 125 at 6% for $\frac{1}{2}$ year
   c. 220 at 5% for 6 months
   d. 160 at 6% for 6 months
   e. $480 at 5% for 3 months
   f. 300 at 6% for 3 months
   g. 600 at 5% for 2 months
   h. 150 at 6% for 2 months

4. Henry borrowed $275 from a friend for two years at 6% per year. How much money must he repay at the end of the two years?

5. John borrowed $130 from a friend for 6 months at 5% interest. How much would he have to pay his friend at the end of the 6 months?

SECTION 2   60-Day Method of Finding Interest

Class Drill

1. Find 6% of $134
2. Find 5% of $117
3. Find 6% of $143.25
4. Find 6% of $275.15
5. Find 5% of $82.26
6. Find $\frac{1}{2}$ of $23.70
7. Find $\frac{1}{4}$ of $17.60
8. Find $\frac{1}{6}$ of $24.10
9. Find $\frac{1}{2}$ of $37.50
10. Find $\frac{1}{4}$ of $15.75

Sample Problem

Find the interest on a loan of $350 for 30 days at 6%.

Explanation

In order to find the interest for 60 days at 6% interest, a short-cut method may be used. Since there are 360 days in a year for interest calculation, a 60 day loan is for 60/360 part of a year, which may be reduced to 1/6. If the interest rate is 6%, then 1/6 of 6% equals a 1% rate for 60 days. To find the interest for 30 days, which is 1/2 of 60 days, first find the interest for 60 days, then find 1/2 of the result.

Sample Solution

$350 for 30 days at 6%
$3.50 for 60 days at 6%
$1.75 for 30 days at 6%

Notes

1. To find the interest for 60 days at 6% on any amount, move the decimal point two places to the left.

2. To find the interest for 30 days, take 1/2 of the amount for 60 days.

3. To find the interest for 90 days, add the interest for 60 days and the interest for 30 days.

4. To find the interest for 15 days, take 1/4 of the amount for 60 days.

Problems

1. Find the interest on the following amounts at 6%:
   a. $145 for 60 days
   b. 234 for 60 days
   c. 117.60 for 60 days
   d. 127.43 for 60 days
   e. $140 for 30 days
   f. 260 for 30 days
   g. 185.50 for 30 days
   h. 275.80 for 30 days

2. Find the interest on the following amounts at 6%:
   a. $162 for 30 days
   b. 52 for 15 days
   c. 136 for 15 days
   d. 238 for 90 days
   e. 62 for 90 days
   f. $244 for 45 days
   g. 152 for 45 days
   h. 235 for 90 days
   i. 347 for 90 days
   j. 252 for 45 days

3. Find the interest on the following amounts at 6%:
   a. $170 for 66 days
   b. 250 for 66 days
   c. 150 for 54 days
   d. 370 for 54 days
   e. 160 for 96 days
   f. 130 for 96 days
   g. $140 for 33 days
   h. 260 for 33 days
   i. 120 for 27 days
   j. 380 for 27 days
   k. 270 for 12 days
   l. 150 for 12 days

4. Find the interest on the following amounts, using the 60 day method:
   Notes: 1. To find the interest at 5%, first find the interest at 6% for the required number of days, then deduct 1/6 of the answer.
   2. To find the interest at 4%, first find the interest at 6% for the required number of days, then deduct 2/6 or 1/3 of the answer.
   a. $144 for 60 days at 5%
   b. 282 for 60 days at 5%
   c. 348 for 30 days at 5%
   d. 372 for 30 days at 5%
   e. 480 for 90 days at 5%
   f. 264 for 90 days at 5%
   g. $126 for 60 days at 4%
   h. 174 for 60 days at 4%
   i. 330 for 30 days at 4%
   j. 546 for 30 days at 4%
   k. 270 for 90 days at 4%
   l. 150 for 90 days at 4%

SECTION 3   Finding Maturity Value of Notes .

Class Drill

Find the interest at 6% on each of the following amounts, using the 60-day method:

1. $250 for 60 days
2.   345 for 60 days
3.   140 for 30 days
4.   260 for 30 days

5. $120 for 90 days
6.   160 for 90 days
7.   240 for 45 days
8.   160 for 45 days

Sample Problem

Mr. Hamilton borrowed $150 from a friend on March 6, and agreed to repay the loan, plus 6% interest, in 30 days.
a. When must the loan be repaid?
b. How much must be repaid?

Explanation

When money is borrowed, the person who borrows usually signs a promissory note to show the amount of the loan, the interest rate, and when the loan, plus the interest, will be repaid. Here is a typical note:

> $ 150 00/100   New York, N.Y. *March 6, 197___*
>
> *Thirty days*   after date *I*   promise to pay to the order
>
> of *John Stern*
>
> *One hundred fifty and 00/100* Dollars
>
> Payable at *Second National Bank*
>
> Value received with interest at *6%*
>
> No. *5* Due *April 5, 197___* *George Hamilton*

The date when the note must be paid is called the "due date," or the "date of maturity" of the note. The amount to be paid on the due date is called the "maturity value" of the note.

Sample Solution

a. Long way: March 6–March 31 = 25 days
            April 1–5   = 5 days   The due date is April 5.
                             30 days

Short way: 30 days from March 6 would be April 5.

b. $150 for 30 days at 6% $150.00 Amount of note
   1.50 for 60 days at 6%   .75 Interest for 30 days
    .75 for 30 days at 6%   150.75 Maturity value of note

Explanation

To find the due date the long way, count from the date of the note to the end of the month, then add additional days in the next month or months to reach the number of days needed.

To count the short way, look at the notes on page 15. However, if a loan is for one month instead of 30 days, the due date will be the same date in the next month.

Examples: 30 days from May 5 = June 4
One month from May 5 = June 5

Problems

1. Jim Steele borrowed $140 from his friend on April 6. He agreed to pay the money back in 30 days, plus 6% interest.
   a. When must the loan be paid back?
   b. How much must be paid on the due date?

2. On July 7, Bill Siegel gave his friend a 30-day promissory note for $300 with interest at 6%.
   a. What is the maturity date of the note?
   b. What is the maturity value of the note?

3. Dan Mathews borrowed $350 from his friend on March 17. He gave his friend a promissory note for 60 days with interest at 6%.
   a. When must the loan be paid back?
   b. How much money must be paid at the end of 60 days?

4. Charlie borrowed $200 from his friend on August 8, and agreed to return the money, plus 6% interest, in 60 days.
   a. By what date must Charlie return the money?
   b. How much must Charlie pay on the due date?

5-10. Find (a) the date of maturity, and (b) the maturity value for each of these notes:

	Date of Note	Amount of Note	Time of Note	Interest Rate
5.	June 18	$475	60 days	6%
6.	September 14	$150	30 days	6%
7.	December 4	$175	2 months	6%
8.	January 10	$250	1 month	6%
9.	March 17	$240	2 months	5%
10.	October 21	$375	2 months	4%

SECTION 4   Discounting Notes

Class Drill

Find the interest on each of the following loans using the 60 day method:

1. $150 for 60 days at 6%
2. $ 45 for 60 days at 6%
3. $128 for 30 days at 6%
4. $170 for 30 days at 6%
5. $240 for 15 days at 5%
6. $160 for 90 days at 6%
7. $250 for 90 days at 6%
8. $300 for 60 days at 5%
9. $240 for 60 days at 4%
10. $ 75 for 60 days at 4%

Sample Problem   Mr. Stern decided to borrow from a bank instead of going to his friend for a loan. He borrowed $500 for 60 days. If the bank's interest rate for money that it lends is 6%, how much will the bank charge for the loan, and how much money will Mr. Stern receive?

Explanation   When a bank lends money, the interest that it charges is called the "bank discount", and the rate is called the "discount rate". The bank discount is deducted by the bank in advance. Notice that the procedure is different from that followed when you borrow money from an individual, because the interest on a loan from an individual is paid at the end when the loan is paid back. (See sample problem and solution on page 34.)

Sample Solution

$500 Loan
   5 Bank Discount
$495 Cash Received (or Net Proceeds)

Problems

1. Mr. Clancy borrowed $450 at the bank at 6% for 60 days. How much did Mr. Clancy receive from the bank?

2. Mr. Burns discounted his $740 note at the bank at a discount rate of 6%. The note was for 60 days. How much were the net proceeds?

3. Harry Thomas discounted at 6% his $150 60-day note. Find the net proceeds.

4. George Daniel discounted his 90-day $450 note at a 6% discount rate. What were the net proceeds?

5-10. Find (a) the date of maturity, and (b) the net proceeds of each of the following notes that were discounted at a bank at 6% discount rate:

	Date of Note	Amount of Note	Time of Note
5.	April 14	$225	60 days
6.	May 29	$143	60 days
7.	July 17	$140	30 days
8.	November 9	$450	30 days
9.	August 17	$125	60 days
10.	October 25	$275	60 days

SECTION 5   Compound Interest

Class Drill

1. Find 1% of $170
2. Find 1% of $250
3. Find 1% of $145
4. Find 10% of $140
5. Find 10% of $250

6. Multiply 75 by 10
7. Divide 42 by 10
8. Divide 650 by 100
9. Find 1% of $147
10. Find 1% of $ 25

Mr. Smith deposited $200 in the Union Savings Bank on July 1. The bank pays interest at 4% per annum compounded quarterly. How much will Mr. Smith have on deposit by December 31, if he does not deposit or withdraw any money?

Savings banks pay "compound interest." This means that interest will be computed for the first interest period on the original amount deposited, but during each subsequent period the interest will be computed on the original deposit plus interest that has been earned. "Compounded quarterly" means that the bank will figure the interest each three months, usually at the end of March, June, September and December. The 4% rate is "per annum," which means for a full year; for three months, the rate will be $\frac{1}{4}$ as much, or 1% for each quarter of the year. The bank figures interest on whole dollars, not on cents.

$200.00 Deposit on July 1
    2.00 Interest for July, August, September
  202.00 Balance September 30
    2.02 Interest for October, November, December
$204.02 Balance on December 31

1. Mr. David deposited $500 in a savings bank on April 1. If the bank pays 4% interest per annum, compounded quarterly, what will be the balance on October 1, if Mr. David makes no further deposits or withdrawals?

2. Mr. Watson deposited $150 in a savings bank on April 1. If the bank pays 4% interest compounded quarterly, what will be the balance on December 31?

3. In each of the following problems, find the savings bank balance on the date shown, assuming the bank pays interest at 4% per annum compounded quarterly:

	Date of Deposit	Amount of Deposit	Find Balance on:
a)	October 1	$350	April 1
b)	July 1	700	April 1
c)	January 2	450	December 31
d)	January 2	340	December 31

4. On April 1 Mr. Reilly deposited $300 in a savings bank paying 4% interest compounded quarterly. On July 1 Mr. Reilly deposited another $200. What was his balance on October 1?

5. Mr. Benson deposited $250 in a savings bank on July 1. The bank pays 4% interest compounded quarterly. On October 1 Mr. Benson deposited $200 more. What was his balance on December 31?

6. Sam Mates deposited $200 in a savings bank on April 1. The bank pays 5% interest, compounded quarterly. What will be the balance on October 1? (Note: multiply by .05, then divide by 4, to find quarterly interest.)

7. In each of the following problems, find the savings bank balance on the date shown, assuming the bank compounds interest quarterly:

	Date of Deposit	Amount of Deposit	Interest Rate	Find Balance on:
a)	July 1	$600	5%	December 31
b)	October 1	500	5%	April 1
c)	April 1	450	4%	
	July 1	100	4%	October 1
d)	October 1	700	4%	
	January 2	200	4%	April 1

SECTION 6   Review Problems

1. What is the interest for 1 year at 5% on $450?

2. Find the interest on $240 for 3 years at 6%.

3. Use the 60-day method of finding interest for each of the following:
   a. $160 for 60 days at 6%
   b. $125.75 for 60 days at 6%
   c. $180 for 30 days at 6%
   d. $ 70 for 90 days at 6%
   e. $320 for 45 days at 6%
   f. $180 for 60 days at 5%
   g. $ 75 for 60 days at 4%

4. Tony borrowed $50 from his friend on October 15, and agreed to return the money, with interest of 6%, in 60 days.
   a. By what date must Tony return the money?
   b. How much must Tony pay on the due date?

5. Mr. Steele discounted his $250 note at the bank at a discount rate of 6%. The note was dated November 12, and was for 60 days.
   a. How much cash did Mr. Steele receive from the bank on November 12?
   b. On what date must the note be paid?
   c. How much must be paid on the due date?

6. Mr. Hartley deposited $350 in a savings bank paying 4% interest. He deposited the money on April 1. Interest is compounded quarterly.
   a. What is the balance on July 1?
   b. What is the balance on October 1?
   c. What is the balance on January 1?

38

7. Mr. Aaron deposited $600 on April 1 in a savings bank paying 4% interest, compounded quarterly. On October 1 he deposited another $300.
   a. Find his balance on July 1.
   b. Find his balance on January 1.

8. Ed deposited $300 in a savings bank on July 1. The bank pays 5% interest, compounded quarterly.
   a. What is the balance on October 1?
   b. What is the balance on January 1?

UNIT 4

Payroll

Computing Earnings at Hourly Rate

Class Drill

Add:

	1.		2.		3.		4.		5.	Multiply:
	8		8		$7\frac{1}{4}$		8		$7\frac{1}{4}$	6. 1.60×40
	8		$7\frac{1}{2}$		$7\frac{1}{2}$		$6\frac{1}{2}$		$6\frac{1}{4}$	7. 1.45×40
	7		7		8		$7\frac{3}{4}$		$7\frac{1}{2}$	8. 1.70×38
	8		$8\frac{1}{2}$		$7\frac{1}{2}$		8		8	9. $1.80 \times 36\frac{1}{2}$
	8		8		8		8		8	10. $1.60 \times 35\frac{1}{4}$

Sample Problem

Mr. Sullivan works for the Empire Supply Company. His time card for the week appears at the left below.

Mr. Sullivan			
In	Out	In	Out
M. 8:00	12:00	1:00	5:00
T. 7:58	12:00	12:59	5:01
W. 7:59	12:02	12:58	5:02
Th. 8:07	12:00	12:59	5:01
F. 8:20	12:00	1:07	5:00

Workers in this firm are supposed to work during the morning from 8 A.M. to 12:00 Noon, and during the afternoon from 1 P.M. to 5 P.M. Any lateness up to 15 minutes costs the worker 15 minutes pay; any lateness from 16 minutes to 30 minutes costs the worker 30 minutes pay; etc.

If Mr. Sullivan earns $2.20 an hour, how much did he earn for the week?

Explanation

Employers can tell how many hours each employee worked by looking at the time card. In this case Mr. Sullivan worked 8 hours on Monday, 8 hours on Tuesday, and 8 hours on Wednesday. Note that the employer does not pay for the extra minute or two shown on the time card before 8 A.M., after 12:00 Noon, before 1 P.M., or after 5 P.M. On Thursday Mr. Sullivan arrived 7 minutes late, and is penalized 15 minutes pay; he therefore earned $7\frac{3}{4}$

41

hours pay. On Friday he was late 20 minutes in the morning, and therefore lost 30 minutes pay; he was late 7 minutes in the afternoon, and therefore lost 15 minutes pay. On Friday, therefore, he earned pay for $7\frac{1}{4}$ hours.

Sample Solution

<u>Hours</u> <u>Worked</u>

	A.M.	P.M.	Total
Monday	4	4	8
Tuesday	4	4	8
Wednesday	4	4	8
Thursday	$3\frac{3}{4}$	4	$7\frac{3}{4}$
Friday	$3\frac{1}{2}$	$3\frac{3}{4}$	$7\frac{1}{4}$

$38\frac{4}{4} = 1$
$= 39$ hours

```
$2.20  Rate per hour
 ×39   Hours
 1980
 660
$85.80 Earned
```

Problems

1. Time cards for other workers in the Empire Supply Co. (see sample problem) are shown below:

Mr. Ahern Rate $2.00 an hour			
In	Out	In	Out
M. 8:00	12:00	1:00	5:00
T. 7:57	12:00	1:00	5:02
W. 8:06	12:01	12:59	5:01
Th. 7:59	12:02	12:58	5:00
F. 8:05	12:00	1:00	5:01

Mr. Brophy Rate $3.00 an hour			
In	Out	In	Out
M. 7:59	12:00	1:00	5:01
T. 8:00	12:01	12:59	5:00
W. 7:58	12:02	1:07	5:01
Th. 8:10	12:00	12:58	5:00
F. 8:00	12:02	12:59	5:01

Mr. Callahan Rate $3.00 an hour			
In	Out	In	Out
M. 7:58	12:01	12:59	5:02
T. 8:12	12:02	12:58	5:01
W. 7:59	12:00	1:08	5:01
Th. 8:00	12:03	12:57	5:02
F. 8:18	12:01	12:59	5:00

Mr. Dempsey Rate $2.00 an hour			
In	Out	In	Out
M. 8:00	12:02	12:59	5:02
T. 7:59	12:01	1:09	5:01
W. 8:05	12:00	12:59	5:00
Th. 8:12	12:01	12:58	5:01
F. 8:17	12:00	12:59	5:00

For each worker, find: a) the number of hours worked daily and for the week.
b) the amount earned for the week.

2. The following students worked part time in a supermarket. According to their time cards, they worked the hours shown at the rates indicated.

	M	T	W	Th	F	Rate
Al	4	3	3	3	4	$2.50
Bill	3	4	3	5	2	2.60
Charlie	2	$4\frac{1}{2}$	3	5	2	2.00
Dan	3	3	$4\frac{1}{2}$	3	5	3.00
Ed	4	3	4	4	3	2.45
Fred	5	4	5	4	4	2.45

a. How many hours did each work during the week?

b. How much did each earn for the week?

3. According to the time cards the employees of a firm worked as shown below, and were paid the hourly rates shown:

	M	T	W	Th	F	Rate
Mr. Fraser	7	8	7	8	7	$3.23
Mr. Gregory	$7\frac{1}{2}$	8	$7\frac{1}{4}$	8	8	4.00
Mr. Harris	8	$6\frac{1}{4}$	$7\frac{1}{4}$	8	$7\frac{1}{2}$	2.62
Mrs. Ivers	$7\frac{1}{4}$	8	7	8	8	3.00

a. How many hours did each work during the week?

b. How much did each earn for the week?

SECTION 2   Computing Overtime Earnings

Class Drill

Multiply:
1. $1.60 × 39
2. $1.75 × 38
3. $2.35 × 40
4. $2.65 × 40
5. $1.50 × $3\frac{1}{2}$
6. $1.60 × $2\frac{1}{2}$
7. $1.80 × $4\frac{1}{2}$
8. $1.60 × $3\frac{1}{2}$

Sample Problem

Mr. Sullivan worked 44 hours during the week. If he earned $2.20 an hour, how much did he earn for the week?

Explanation

Federal law requires that firms engaged in interstate commerce pay time-and-one-half to any employee who has worked more than 40 hours in a week. This means that for every hour worked over 40 hours, the firm must pay an extra one-half hour's pay. Many firms also follow this practice even if they are not covered by the law, because they have signed an agreement with the union. We shall follow the regulation in all problems.

Sample Solution

```
                 44 hours worked          $2.20  rate per hour
               - 40 hours                  ×40  hours
                  4 hours overtime       $88.00  Regular pay
  ½ × 4 =        2 bonus for overtime
                  6 hours pay for overtime $2.20  rate per hour
                                            ×6  hours paid for overtime
                                         $13.20  Overtime Pay
```

$88.00 Regular Pay
 13.20 Overtime Pay
$101.20 Total Pay

43

Notes

> To find pay when a man has worked overtime:
>
> 1. Subtract 40 hours from hours worked to find overtime hours. Find $\frac{1}{2}$ of the overtime hours to find overtime bonus, and add to find total hours earned for overtime.
>
> 2. Multiply regular rate by 40 to find regular pay.
>
> 3. Multiply regular rate by overtime hours found in (1) to find overtime pay.
>
> 4. Add regular pay and overtime pay to find total pay.

Problems

1. Mr. Ahern worked 42 hours during the week. If he earned $2.00 an hour, how much did he earn for the week? (In all problems, use time-and-one-half for any overtime hours over 40)

2. Mr. Brophy worked 46 hours during the week. How much did he earn, if he worked at $3.00 an hour?

3. Mr. Callahan worked 45 hours for the week. What did he earn, if he worked at a rate of $2.00 an hour?

4. Mr. Dempsey worked 43 hours during the week, and earned $3.00 an hour. How much did he earn for the week?

5. The following employees worked as shown below. Find the amount each employee earned for the week.

	Hours Worked	Rate per Hour
Mr. Fraser	46	$2.23
Mr. Gregory	45	2.00
Mr. Harris	44	2.62
Mr. Iver	41	3.00
Mr. Jordan	42	2.35
Mr. Keily	43	3.00
Mr. Lamonte	48	2.38
Mr. Mullins	47	3.00

SECTION 3   Annual Salary

Class Drill

Multiply:

1. $2.45 × 40
2. $1.75 × 12
3. $2.30 × 40
4. $2.15 × 8
5. $2.50 × $5\frac{1}{2}$

6. 240 × $.50
7. 135 × $.50
8. 1,247 × $.10
9. 352 × $.25
10. 785 × $.10

Sample Problem

Mr. Stevens earns $5,000 a year.
   a. How much does he earn each month? (to the nearest cent)
   b. How much does he earn each week? (to the nearest cent)

Sample Solution

$$\frac{416.666}{12)\ 5,000.000} = \$416.67 \text{ a month}$$

$$\frac{96.153}{52)\ 5,000.000} = \$96.15 \text{ a week}$$

```
          96.153  = $96.15 a week
52) 5,000.000
    4 68
      320
      312
       8 0
       5 2
       2 80
       2 60
         200
         156
```

Notes

1. To find the answer to the nearest cent, carry the division to three decimal places. If the third decimal place is a 5 or higher, change the answer to the next cent; if it is a 4 or lower, drop it.

2. Use short division when divisor is 12 or less.

Problems

1. Mr. Landers has a yearly salary of $6,000.
   a. What is his monthly salary?
   b. What is his weekly salary?

2. Harry Jenkins earns $4,500 a year.
   a. How much does he earn a month?
   b. How much does he earn a week?

3. Each of the following men is on an annual salary. For each, find:
   a. the amount earned each month.
   b. the amount earned each week.

Mr. Nevins	$ 5,700
Mr. Owens	7,500
Mr. Pine	6,200
Mr. Roberts	10,000

4. Bill Sanders earns $120 a week for a regular 40 hour week.
   a. How much does he earn an hour?
   b. If he worked 44 hours one week, how much did he earn?

5. Howard Stevens earns $100 a week for 40 hours.
   a. How much does he earn an hour?
   b. If he worked 46 hours one week, how much did he earn?

6. George Bellows earns $160 for a 40-hour week. Last week he took off a day for personal business, and was not paid for the day.
   a. How much does he earn an hour?
   b. How much did he earn last week?

7. Dan McGee earns $140 for a 40-hour week. Last week he took off half a day for personal business, for which he was not paid.
   a. How much does he earn an hour?
   b. How much did he earn last week?

SECTION 4   Commission

Class Drill

1. Find 10% of $ 457
2. Find 1% of $3,256
3. Find 10% of $ 474
4. Find 25% of $ 328
5. Find 50% of $ 127

6. Find $32 × 10
7. Find $29.70 × 10
8. Add $426 and $35
9. Add $125 and $6.43
10. Add $17.52 and $136

Sample Problem

George Loring, a salesman, receives a salary of $35 a week plus a commission of 10% on sales. If he sold $470 worth of goods during the week, what was the total amount he earned?

Explanation

Business firms use various methods to encourage salesmen to do their best. Some firms pay salesmen a fixed amount for each item sold; some pay a percent of the sales; some pay a salary plus commission; some increase the rates when the salesmen sell more than a certain amount.

Sample Solution

10% of $470 is $47 commission

$35 Salary
 47 Commission
$82 Total Earned

Problems

1. Al receives 10¢ for each magazine he sells. If he sold 125 during the week, how much did he earn?

2. Mr. Gorden is paid a commission of $1.25 for each item he sells. If he sold 88 items during the week, what did he earn?

46

3. Bill receives a commission of 25% of sales. If he sold $652 worth of goods during the week, how much did he earn?

4. Barry is paid 50% of all sales. If he sold $259.76 worth of merchandise, what was his commission?

5. Mr. Gray receives a salary of $40 a week plus a commission of 20% on sales. If he sold $350 worth of goods during the week, how much did he earn for the week?

6. Mr. Delano receives a salary of $30 a week plus a commission of 25% on sales. If his sales for the week were $465, how much did he earn?

7. Mr. Seymour receives a salary of $50 a week plus a 10% commission on sales over $500 during the week. The 10% applies only to the amount in excess of $500. For example, if he sold $600 worth of goods, he would earn a 10% commission on $100, which is the amount in excess of $500.

Find his total earnings during each of the following weeks:

First week: Sales $ 450
Second week: Sales $ 600
Third week: Sales $ 850
Fourth week: Sales $1,220

8. Mr. Celler sells vacuum cleaners. He receives a commission of $6 for each cleaner he sells up to five; if he sells 6 to 10 cleaners he receives a commission of $9 each; if he sells 11 or more he receives $12 for each one sold. Find his commission during each of the following weeks:

First week: 4 cleaners sold
Second week: 8 cleaners sold ($9 applies above 5 only)
Third week: 11 cleaners sold ($12 applies above 10 only)
Fourth week: 15 cleaners sold

9. Mr. Baskind works as a salesman for the following commissions:

Sales up to $500   8% commission
Sales in excess of $500 up to $1,000   12% added to above
Sales in excess of $1,000   15% added to above

Find his commission during each week:

First week: Sales $ 400
Second week: Sales $ 600
Third week: Sales $ 900
Fourth week: Sales $1,200

SECTION 5   Finding Take-Home Pay: Social Security Tax

Class Drill

1. Find 4% of $250
2. Find 4% of $175
3. Find 5% of $220
4. Find 5% of $190
5. Find 4% of $215

6. Find 5.85% (.0585) of $70
7. Find 5.85% of $90
8. Find 5.85% of $100
9. Find 5.85% of $200
10. Find 5.85% of $130

Sample Problem

John earns $80 a week. How much will be taken out of his pay for the social security tax? How much cash will he receive?

Explanation

During their working years, employees pay social security (F.I.C.A.) taxes which go into special funds to provide these benefits later on:

a) *Retirement benefits* — paid to men and women after they retire.

b) *Survivors benefits* — after the worker dies, paid to the widow at age 60, to his unmarried children under 18, to the widow at any age if she is caring for a child under 18, and to dependent parents 62 or over.

c) *Disability benefits* — paid to worker before 65 if he has a severe disability lasting at least 12 months, to disabled widow of worker, to disabled children of worker who died.

d) *Health insurance* (medicare) — paid to men and women 65 or older for: 1) hospital expenses; 2) medical expenses, if person agrees to pay a monthly premium. The premium in 1973 was $5.80 a month from January through August and $6.30 a month for the remaining four months of the year. Medical payments cover 80% of reasonable charges, except for the first $60 a year.

The worker pays 5.85% of his salary on earnings up to $10,800 during 1973, and on earnings up to $13,200 during 1974. This social security tax is deducted from the pay of the worker, and is matched by his employer. The amount paid to the worker, after deducting the tax, is called his "take-home" pay.

Sample Solution

Salary	$80	or	.0585		$80.00	Salary
	× .0585		× 80		4.68	S.S. Tax
	400		4.6800 = $4.68		$75.32	Take-home Pay
	640					
	400					
	4.6800 = $4.68					

48

Problems

1. George earns $90 a week. Find a) his social security tax

   b) his take-home pay

2. For each of the following employees, find the social security tax and the take-home pay for the week:

	Salary
Al	$70
Bill	60
Charlie	85
Dan	95
Ed	84
Fred	97

3. Find the social security tax for each man.

	Wage
Mr. Ahern	$87
Mr. Brophy	62
Mr. Callahan	50
Mr. Dempsey	75
Mr. Eagers	82
Mr. Fraser	95
Mr. Gregory	110

SECTION 6   Social Security Tax: Use of Tax Tables

Class Drill

1. Find 5.85% of $60

2. Find 5.85% of $130

3. Find 5.85% of $200

4. Find 5.85% of $150

5. Find 1% of $455

6. Find 10% of $175

7. Find 25% of $48

8. Find 50% of $46

Sample Problem

The payroll clerk of a company wishes to find the social security tax on these employees very quickly:

Mr. A Salary $90.00
Mr. B Salary $90.20
Mr. C Salary $123.75

What quick method does he use?

49

Explanation

The Internal Revenue Service provides tax tables for employers so that payroll clerks may find the social security tax quickly. Here is a *portion* of the table as it appeared on January 1, 1973.

Social Security Employee Tax Table—Continued

5.85 percent employee tax deductions

Wages		Tax to be withheld	Wages		Tax to be withheld	Wages		Tax to be withheld	Wages		Tax to be withheld
At least	But less than		At least	But less than		At least	But less than		At least	But less than	
$88.81	$88.98	$5.20	$99.92	$100.09	$5.85	$111.03	$111.20	$6.50	$122.14	$122.31	$7.15
88.98	89.15	5.21	100.09	100.26	5.86	111.20	111.37	6.51	122.31	122.48	7.16
89.15	89.32	5.22	100.26	100.43	5.87	111.37	111.54	6.52	122.48	122.65	7.17
89.32	89.49	5.23	100.43	100.60	5.88	111.54	111.71	6.53	122.65	122.83	7.18
89.49	89.66	5.24	100.60	100.77	5.89	111.71	111.89	6.54	122.83	123.00	7.19
89.66	89.83	5.25	100.77	100.95	5.90	111.89	112.06	6.55	123.00	123.17	7.20
89.83	90.00	5.26	100.95	101.12	5.91	112.06	112.23	6.56	123.17	123.34	7.21
90.00	90.18	5.27	101.12	101.29	5.92	112.23	112.40	6.57	123.34	123.51	7.22
90.18	90.35	5.28	101.29	101.46	5.93	112.40	112.57	6.58	123.51	123.68	7.23
90.35	90.52	5.29	101.46	101.63	5.94	112.57	112.74	6.59	123.68	123.85	7.24
90.52	90.69	5.30	101.63	101.80	5.95	112.74	112.91	6.60	123.85	124.02	7.25
90.69	90.86	5.31	101.80	101.97	5.96	112.91	113.08	6.61	124.02	124.19	7.26
90.86	91.03	5.32	101.97	102.14	5.97	113.08	113.25	6.62	124.19	124.36	7.27
91.03	91.20	5.33	102.14	102.31	5.98	113.25	113.42	6.63	124.36	124.53	7.28
91.20	91.37	5.34	102.31	102.48	5.99	113.42	113.59	6.64	124.53	124.71	7.29
91.37	91.54	5.35	102.48	102.65	6.00	113.59	113.77	6.65	124.71	124.88	7.30
91.54	91.71	5.36	102.65	102.83	6.01	113.77	113.94	6.66	124.88	125.05	7.31
91.71	91.89	5.37	102.83	103.00	6.02	113.94	114.11	6.67	125.05	125.22	7.32
91.89	92.06	5.38	103.00	103.17	6.03	114.11	114.28	6.68	125.22	125.39	7.33
92.06	92.23	5.39	103.17	103.34	6.04	114.28	114.45	6.69	125.39	125.56	7.34
92.23	92.40	5.40	103.34	103.51	6.05	114.45	114.62	6.70	125.56	125.73	7.35
92.40	92.57	5.41	103.51	103.68	6.06	114.62	114.79	6.71	125.73	125.90	7.36
92.57	92.74	5.42	103.68	103.85	6.07	114.79	114.96	6.72	125.90	126.07	7.37
			103.85	104.02	6.08	114.96	115.13	6.73			7.38
						115.13	115.30				

Sample Solution

Mr. A: Salary $90.00 is at least $90.00 but less than $90.18. Tax is $5.27.

Mr. B: Salary $90.20 is at least $90.18 but less than $90.35. Tax is $5.28.

Mr. C: Salary $123.75 is at least $123.68 but less than $123.85. Tax is $7.24.

In each of the following problems first find the social security tax by multiplying by the tax rate of 5.85% (.0585), then check your answer by using the table.

1. Salary $100

2. Salary $115

3. Salary $123

4. Salary $124

5. Salary $91

6. Salary $101

7. Salary $103

8. Salary $112

SECTION 7   Finding Take-Home Pay: Federal Withholding Tax

Class Drill

1. Find 5.85% of $120

2. Find 5.85% of $90

3. Find 5.85% of $85

4. Find 5.85% of $130

5. Add: $ 8.55 + $ 7.40 + $ 6.20

6. Add: $13.50 + $ 6.25 + $ 9.51

7. Add: $17.25 + $ 6.42 + $18.50

8. Add: $ 6.48 + $17.50 + $ 4.19

Sample Problem

John earns $80 a week. He is single. How much will be taken out of his pay for federal income (withholding) tax?

Explanation

The federal government requires each employer to withhold from the pay of each employee a certain amount of money each pay day as part payment of the employee's federal income tax. In this way each employee pays some of his income tax each time he is paid, instead of paying the entire tax when he sends in his federal income tax return not later than April 15. The tax taken out of his pay is called the "federal withholding tax."

The amount of withholding tax is based on the salary of the employee, and the number of "allowances". The employer determines the allowances by having each employee fill out an "Employee's Withholding Allowance Certificate", Form W-4, shown on page 52.

Look at Form W-4. You will see that the employee may claim one allowance for himself, one for his wife, one for each dependent, and extra allowances for age or blindness.

Beginning in 1972, the employee may also claim a "special withholding allowance" (see line h). This special allowance may be claimed by a single person who does not have two or more jobs, and by married persons unless both husband and wife are employed. The purpose of this special allowance is to reduce the amount of the withholding tax for these people, because in the past too much money was taken out of their pay.

Beginning in 1970, an employee who did not pay a federal income tax for the previous year and who does not expect to have any during the current year, may fill out Form W-4E "Exemption from Withholding" instead of Form W-4. This would apply to most students who are working part-time. If Form W-4E is given to the employer, he will not take federal withholding tax out of the pay of the employee. A sample of Form W-4E is shown on page 53.

Employee's Withholding Allowance Certificate

The explanatory material below will help you determine your correct number of withholding allowances, and will indicate whether you should complete the new Form W–4 at the bottom of this page.

How Many Withholding Allowances May You Claim?

Please use the schedule below to determine the number of allowances you may claim for tax withholding purposes. In determining the number, keep in mind these points: If you are single and hold more than one job, you may not claim the same allowances with more than one employer at the same time; If you are married and both you and your wife or husband are employed, you may not claim the same allowances with your employers at the same time. A nonresident alien other than a resident of Canada, Mexico or Puerto Rico may claim only one personal allowance.

Figure Your Total Withholding Allowances Below

(a) Allowance for yourself—enter 1 . . . . `1`

(b) Allowance for your wife (husband)—enter 1 . . . .

(c) Allowance for your age—if 65 or over—enter 1 . . . .

(d) Allowance for your wife's (husband's) age—if 65 or over—enter 1 . . . . . .

(e) Allowance for blindness (yourself)—enter 1 . . . .

(f) Allowance for blindness (wife or husband)—enter 1 . . . .

(g) Allowance(s) for dependent(s)—you are entitled to claim an allowance for each dependent you will be able to claim on your Federal income tax return. Do not include yourself or your wife (husband)* . . . . .

(h) Special withholding allowance—if you have only one job, and do not have a wife or husband who works— enter 1 . . . . `1`

(i) Total—add lines (a) through (h) above . . . . `2`

If you do not plan to itemize deductions on your income tax return, enter the number shown on line (i) on line 1, Form W–4 below. Skip lines (j) and (k).

(j) Allowance(s) for itemized deductions—If you do plan to itemize deductions on your income tax return, enter the number from line 5 of worksheet on back . . . .

(k) Total—add lines (i) and (j) above. Enter here and on line 1, Form W–4 below . . . .

*If you are in doubt as to whom you may claim as a dependent, see the instructions which came with your last Federal income tax return or call your local Internal Revenue Service office.

See Table and Worksheet on Back if You Plan to Itemize Your Deductions

Completing New Form W–4

If you find that you are entitled to one or more allowances in addition to those which you are now claiming, please increase your number of allowances by completing the form below and filing with your employer. If the number of allowances you previously claimed decreases, you must file a new Form W–4 within 10 days. (Should you expect to owe more tax than will be withheld, you may use the same form to increase your withholding by claiming fewer or "0" allowances on line 1 or by asking for additional withholding on line 2 or both.)

▼ **Give the bottom part of this form to your employer; keep the upper part for your records and information** ▼

- -

Form W–4
(Rev. Aug. 1972)
Department of the Treasury
Internal Revenue Service

Employee's Withholding Allowance Certificate

(This certificate is for income tax withholding purposes only; it will remain in effect until you change it.)

Type or print your full name
JOHN RICHARDS

Your social security number
304-73-1602

Home address (Number and street or rural route)
25-32 31ST St.

Marital status
☑ Single ☐ Married
(If married but legally separated, or wife (husband) is a nonresident alien, check the single block.)

City or town, State and ZIP code
LONG ISLAND CITY, N.Y. 11102

1 Total number of allowances you are claiming . . . . `2`

2 Additional amount, if any, you want deducted from each pay (if your employer agrees) . . . . `$`

I certify that to the best of my knowledge and belief, the number of withholding allowances claimed on this certificate does not exceed the number to which I am entitled.

Signature ▶ **John Richards**   Date ▶ **Jan. 3**, 19**73**

Exemption From Withholding
(of Federal Income Tax)
**For use by employees who incurred no tax liability
in 1972 and anticipate no tax liability for 1973**

1973

Type or print full name	Social Security Number	Expiration date (see instructions and enter date)

Home address (Number and Street)

City, State, and ZIP Code

Employee.—File this certificate with your employer. Otherwise he must withhold Federal income tax from your wages.

Employer.—Keep this certificate with your records. This certificate may be used instead of Form W–4 by those employees qualified to claim the exemption.

Employee's certification.—Under penalties of perjury, I certify that I incurred no liability for Federal income tax for 1972 and that I anticipate that I will incur no liability for Federal income tax for 1973.

(Signature)

(Date)

The employer finds the amount of the withholding tax by looking at the tables supplied by the government. Separate tables are used for single or married employees. Shown below and on the next page are parts of these tables:

SINGLE Persons—WEEKLY Payroll Period

And the wages are—		And the number of withholding allowances claimed is—										
At least	But less than	0	1	2	3	4	5	6	7	8	9	10 or more
		The amount of income tax to be withheld shall be—										
$80	$82	$12.00	$9.10	$6.50	$3.90	$1.80	$0	$0	$0	$0	$0	$0
82	84	12.40	9.50	6.90	4.30	2.10	0	0	0	0	0	0
84	86	12.80	9.80	7.20	4.60	2.30	.30	0	0	0	0	0
86	88	13.20	10.20	7.60	5.00	2.60	.60	0	0	0	0	0
88	90	13.60	10.60	8.00	5.40	2.90	.90	0	0	0	0	0
90	92	14.10	11.00	8.30	5.70	3.20	1.20	0	0	0	0	0
92	94	14.50	11.40	8.70	6.10	3.50	1.40	0	0	0	0	0
94	96	14.90	11.90	9.00	6.40	3.90	1.70	0	0	0	0	0
96	98	15.30	12.30	9.40	6.80	4.20	2.00	0	0	0	0	0
98	100	15.70	12.70	9.80	7.20	4.60	2.30	.30	0	0	0	0
100	105	16.50	13.40	10.40	7.80	5.20	2.80	.80	0	0	0	0
105	110	17.50	14.50	11.50	8.70	6.10	3.50	1.50	0	0	0	0
110	115	18.60	15.50	12.50	9.60	7.00	4.40	2.20	.10	0	0	0
115	120	19.60	16.60	13.60	10.50	7.90	5.30	2.90	.80	0	0	0
120	125	20.70	17.60	14.60	11.60	8.80	6.20	3.60	1.50	0	0	0
125	130	21.70	18.70	15.70	12.60	9.70	7.10	4.50	2.20	.20	0	0
130	135	22.80	19.70	16.70	13.70	10.70	8.00	5.40	2.90	.90	0	0
135	140	23.80	20.80	17.80	14.70	11.70	8.90	6.30	3.70	1.60	0	0
140	145	24.90	21.80	18.80	15.80	12.80	9.80	7.20	4.60	2.30	.30	0
145	150	25.90	22.90	19.90	16.80	13.80	10.80	8.10	5.50	3.00	1.00	0

MARRIED Persons — WEEKLY Payroll Period

And the wages are—		And the number of withholding allowances claimed is—										
At least	But less than	0	1	2	3	4	5	6	7	8	9	10 or more
		The amount of income tax to be withheld shall be—										
$100	$105	$14.10	$11.80	$9.50	$7.20	$4.90	$2.80	$.80	$0	$0	$0	$0
105	110	14.90	12.60	10.30	8.00	5.70	3.50	1.50	0	0	0	0
110	115	15.70	13.40	11.10	8.80	6.50	4.20	2.20	.10	0	0	0
115	120	16.50	14.20	11.90	9.60	7.30	5.00	2.90	.80	0	0	0
120	125	17.30	15.00	12.70	10.40	8.10	5.80	3.60	1.50	0	0	0
125	130	18.10	15.80	13.50	11.20	8.90	6.60	4.30	2.20	.20	0	0
130	135	18.90	16.60	14.30	12.00	9.70	7.40	5.10	2.90	.90	0	0
135	140	19.70	17.40	15.10	12.80	10.50	8.20	5.90	3.60	1.60	0	0
140	145	20.50	18.20	15.90	13.60	11.30	9.00	6.70	4.40	2.30	.30	0
145	150	21.30	19.00	16.70	14.40	12.10	9.80	7.50	5.20	3.00	1.00	0

Sample Solution

John did not file Form W-4E, because last year he made a good deal of money and had to pay an income tax. When he prepared Form W-4, he first used the top part of the form as follows: On line (a) he wrote "1" and on line (h) he wrote "1" because he had only one job. He added to show a total of "2". On the Certificate that he gave to his employer, he wrote "2" as the number of allowances he claimed.

Since John is single, use the table for single persons. His salary is $80. Look at the left hand column, where you will find the line for wages "at least $80, but less than $82". Look across that line to the column for 2 allowances, and you will find the withholding tax: $6.50.

Problems

1. Bill earned $90 last week. He is single, and claimed 1 allowance plus 1 special withholding allowance on his W-4 form. How much should be taken out of his pay for federal withholding tax?

2. Henry earned $85 last week. He is single, and claimed 1 allowance plus 1 special withholding allowance on his W-4 form. How much should be taken out of his pay for federal withholding tax?

3. George earned $120 last week. He is single, and claimed 2 allowances plus 1 special withholding allowance on his W-4 form (he supports his mother). How much should be taken out of his pay for federal withholding tax?

4. Mr. Brown earned $141.75 during the week. He is single and claimed 3 allowances plus 1 special withholding allowance on his W-4 form (he is over 65 and supports his grandson). How much is his federal withholding tax?

54

5. Mr. Harris earned $133 during the week. He is married and claimed 2 allowances plus 1 special withholding allowance, because his wife does not work. How much is his federal withholding tax? (Remember to use the table for married persons.)

6. Mrs. Harris earned $106 during the week. She is married and claimed 0 allowances on her W-4 form (Mr. Harris claimed both allowances). How much should be taken out of her pay for federal withholding tax?

7. Mr. Davis earned $125.50 last week. He is married and claimed 7 allowances on his W-4 form (he supports 5 children). How much is his federal withholding tax?

SECTION 8

New York State and New York City Withholding Taxes: Use of Combined Tax Tables

Class Drill

Add:

1. $ 5.50 + $17.40 + $16.80

2. $12.65 + $18.57 + $ 8.42

3. $ 8.47 + $16.84 + $17.50

4. $ 9.00 + $21.42 + $ 5.00

Subtract:

5. $157.00 - $16.00

6. $146.00 - $85.00

7. $ 87.53 - $16.47

8. $ 64.33 - $18.58

Sample Problem

Joe earns $85 a week. He is single and claims one allowance.
a) How much will be taken out of his pay for New York State and New York City income (withholding) taxes?
b) How much will be taken out of his pay for social security and federal withholding?

Explanation

New York State and New York City have regulations for withholding income taxes similar to the regulations of the federal government. Once again, the employer uses tax tables to find the amount to be withheld, based on the wages and the number of allowances. The term "*exemption*" is also used in addition to the term "allowance". There are not separate tables for single and married persons, however; both are shown in the same table. In New York City there are separate tables for workers who live in New York City (residents) and for those who do not live in New York City (non-residents). The tax on non-residents is smaller than the tax on residents.

You now see that four separate tables must be consulted to find taxes: tables for social security tax, federal withholding tax, N.Y. State withholding tax, N.Y. City withholding tax. To save time tables have been prepared combining all these tables into one table so that all taxes for an employee may be found on one sheet. Part of such a table is shown on the next page.

1973 N.Y.C. COMBINATION TAX CHART – WEEKLY WAGES $80.00 – $139.00

FEDERAL OLD AGE DEDUCTIONS – 5.85%

WAGES FROM	TAX	WAGES FROM	TAX	WAGES FROM	TAX	WAGES FROM	TAX	WAGES FROM	TAX	WAGES FROM	TAX	WAGES FROM	TAX
80.00	4.68	.09	4.69	.26	4.70	.43	4.71	.60	4.72	.77	4.73	.95	4.74
81.00	4.74	.12	4.75	.29	4.76	.46	4.77	.63	4.78	.80	4.79	.97	4.80
82.00	4.80	.14	4.81	.31	4.82	.48	4.83	.65	4.84	.83	4.85		
83.00	4.86	.17	4.87	.34	4.88	.51	4.89	.68	4.90	.85	4.91		
84.00	4.91	.02	4.92	.19	4.93	.36	4.94	.53	4.95	.71	4.96	.88	4.97
85.00	4.97	.05	4.98	.22	4.99	.39	5.00	.56	5.01	.73	5.02	.90	5.03
86.00	5.03	.07	5.04	.24	5.05	.42	5.06	.59	5.07	.76	5.08	.93	5.09
87.00	5.09	.10	5.10	.27	5.11	.44	5.12	.61	5.13	.78	5.14	.95	5.15
88.00	5.15	.12	5.16	.30	5.17	.47	5.18	.64	5.19	.81	5.20	.98	5.21
89.00	5.21	.15	5.22	.32	5.23	.49	5.24	.66	5.25	.83	5.26		
90.00	5.27	.18	5.28	.35	5.29	.52	5.30	.69	5.31	.86	5.32		
91.00	5.32	.03	5.33	.20	5.34	.37	5.35	.54	5.36	.71	5.37	.89	5.38
92.00	5.38	.06	5.39	.23	5.40	.40	5.41	.57	5.42	.74	5.43	.91	5.44
93.00	5.44	.08	5.45	.25	5.46	.42	5.47	.59	5.48	.77	5.49	.94	5.50
94.00	5.50	.11	5.51	.28	5.52	.45	5.53	.62	5.54	.79	5.55	.96	5.56
95.00	5.56	.13	5.57	.30	5.58	.48	5.59	.65	5.60	.82	5.61	.99	5.62
96.00	5.62	.16	5.63	.33	5.64	.50	5.65	.67	5.66	.84	5.67		
97.00	5.67	.01	5.68	.18	5.69	.36	5.70	.53	5.71	.70	5.72	.87	5.73
98.00	5.73	.04	5.74	.21	5.75	.38	5.76	.55	5.77	.71	5.78	.89	5.79
99.00	5.79	.06	5.80	.24	5.81	.41	5.82	.58	5.83	.75	5.84	.92	5.85
100.00	5.85	.09	5.86	.26	5.87	43	5.88	.60	5.89	.77	5.90	.95	5.91
101.00	5.91	.12	5.92	.29	5.93	46	5.94	.63	5.95	.80	5.96	.97	5.97
102.00	5.97	.14	5.98	.31	5.99	48	6.00	.65	6.01	.83	6.02		
103.00	6.03	.17	6.04	.34	6.05	51	6.06	68	6.07	.85	6.08		
104.00	6.08	.02	6.09	.19	6.10	36	6.11	53	6.12	.71	6.13	.88	6.14
105.00	6.14	.05	6.15	.22	6.16	.39	6.17	.56	6.18	.73	6.19	.90	6.20
106.00	6.20	.07	6.21	.24	6.22	.42	6.23	.59	6.24	.76	6.25	.93	6.26
107.00	6.26	.10	6.27	.27	6.28	.44	6.29	.61	6.30	.78	6.31	.95	6.32
108.00	6.32	.12	6.33	.30	6.34	.47	6.35	.64	6.36	.81	6.37	.98	6.38
109.00	6.38	.15	6.39	.32	6.40	.49	6.41	.66	6.42	.83	6.43		
110.00	6.44	.18	6.45	.35	6.46	.52	6.47	.69	6.48	.86	6.49		
111.00	6.49	.03	6.50	.20	6.51	.37	6.52	.54	6.53	.71	6.54	.89	6.55
112.00	6.55	.06	6.56	.23	6.57	.40	6.58	.57	6.59	.74	6.60	.91	6.61
113.00	6.61	.08	6.62	.25	6.63	.42	6.64	.59	6.65	.77	6.66	.94	6.67
114.00	6.67	.11	6.68	.28	6.69	.45	6.70	.62	6.71	.79	6.72	.96	6.73
115.00	6.73	.13	6.74	.30	6.75	.48	6.76	.65	6.77	.82	6.78	.99	6.79
116.00	6.79	.16	6.80	.33	6.81	.50	6.82	.67	6.83	.84	6.84		
117.00	6.84	.01	6.85	.18	6.86	.36	6.87	.53	6.88	.70	6.89	.87	6.90
118.00	6.90	.04	6.91	.21	6.92	.38	6.93	.55	6.94	.71	6.95	.89	6.96
119.00	6.96	.06	6.97	.24	6.98	.41	6.99	.58	7.00	.75	7.01	.92	7.02
120.00	7.02	.09	7.03	.26	7.04	.43	7.05	.60	7.06	.77	7.07	.95	7.08
121.00	7.08	.12	7.09	.29	7.10	.46	7.11	.63	7.12	.80	7.13	.97	7.14
122.00	7.14	.14	7.15	.31	7.16	.48	7.17	.65	7.18	.83	7.19		
123.00	7.20	.17	7.21	.34	7.22	.51	7.23	.68	7.24	.85	7.25		
124.00	7.25	.02	7.26	.19	7.27	.36	7.28	.53	7.29	.71	7.30	.88	7.31
125.00	7.31	.05	7.32	.22	7.33	.39	7.34	.56	7.35	.73	7.36	.90	7.37
126.00	7.37	.07	7.38	.24	7.39	.42	7.40	.59	7.41	.76	7.42	.93	7.43
127.00	7.43	.10	7.44	.27	7.45	.44	7.46	.61	7.47	.78	7.48	.95	7.49
128.00	7.49	.12	7.50	.30	7.51	.47	7.52	.64	7.53	.81	7.54	.98	7.55
129.00	7.55	.15	7.56	.32	7.57	.49	7.58	.66	7.59	.83	7.60		
130.00	7.61	.18	7.62	.35	7.63	.52	7.64	.69	7.65	.86	7.66		
131.00	7.66	.13	7.67	.20	7.68	.37	7.69	.54	7.70	.71	7.71	.89	7.72
132.00	7.72	.06	7.73	.23	7.74	.40	7.75	.57	7.76	.74	7.77	.91	7.78
133.00	7.78	.08	7.79	.25	7.80	.42	7.81	.59	7.82	.77	7.83	.94	7.84
134.00	7.84	.11	7.85	.28	7.86	.45	7.87	.62	7.88	.79	7.89	.96	7.90
135.00	7.90	.13	7.91	.30	7.92	.48	7.93	.65	7.94	.82	7.95	.99	7.96
136.00	7.96	.16	7.97	.33	7.98	.50	7.99	.67	8.00	.84	8.01		
137.00	8.01	.01	8.02	.18	8.03	.36	8.04	.53	8.05	.70	8.06	.87	8.07
138.00	8.07	.04	8.08	.21	8.09	.38	8.10	.55	8.11	.71	8.12	.89	8.13
139.00	8.13	.06	8.14	.24	8.15	.41	8.16	.58	8.17	.75	8.18	.92	8.19

EXEMPTIONS AND WITHHOLDING DEDUCTIONS

WAGES FROM	0				1				2				3				4				5				NYS Dis.	N.Y.C. Comm. Tax
	FEDERAL S	FEDERAL M	State	City	FEDERAL S	FEDERAL M	State	City	FEDERAL S	FEDERAL M	State	City	FEDERAL S	FEDERAL M	State	City	FEDERAL S	FEDERAL M	State	City	FEDERAL S	FEDERAL M	State	City		
80.00	12.00	**10.70**	2.30	.85	9.10	**8.40**	1.70	.70	6.50	**6.10**	1.30	.55	3.90	**3.80**	.90	.40	1.80	**1.80**	.50	.30			.20	.15	.30	.10
81.00	12.00	**10.70**	2.30	.85	9.10	**8.40**	1.70	.70	6.50	**6.10**	1.30	.55	3.90	**3.80**	.90	.40	1.80	**1.80**	.50	.30			.20	.15		
82.00	12.40	**11.00**	2.30	.85	9.50	**8.70**	1.80	.70	6.90	**6.40**	1.40	.55	4.30	**4.10**	1.00	.40	2.10	**2.10**	.60	.30			.30	.15		
83.00	12.40	**11.00**	2.30	.85	9.50	**8.70**	1.80	.70	6.90	**6.40**	1.40	.55	4.30	**4.10**	1.00	.40	2.10	**2.10**	.60	.30	0	**0**	.30	.15		
84.00	12.80	**11.30**	2.40	.90	9.80	**9.00**	1.90	.75	7.20	**6.70**	1.40	.60	4.60	**4.40**	1.10	.45	2.30	**2.30**	.70	.35	.30	**.30**	.30	.20		
85.00	12.80	**11.30**	2.40	.90	9.80	**9.00**	1.90	.75	7.20	**6.70**	1.40	.60	4.60	**4.40**	1.10	.45	2.30	**2.30**	.70	.35	.30	**.30**	.30	.20	.30	.15
86.00	13.20	**11.70**	2.50	.90	10.20	**9.30**	2.00	.75	7.60	**7.00**	1.50	.60	5.00	**4.70**	1.10	.45	2.60	**2.60**	.70	.35	.60	**.60**	.40	.20		
87.00	13.20	**11.70**	2.50	.90	10.20	**9.30**	2.00	.75	7.60	**7.00**	1.50	.60	5.00	**4.70**	1.10	.45	2.60	**2.60**	.70	.35	.60	**.60**	.40	.20		
88.00	13.60	**12.00**	2.60	.95	10.60	**9.70**	2.10	.80	8.00	**7.40**	1.60	.65	5.40	**5.00**	1.20	.50	2.90	**2.90**	.80	.35	.90	**.90**	.40	.25		
89.00	13.60	**12.00**	2.60	.95	10.60	**9.70**	2.10	.80	8.00	**7.40**	1.60	.65	5.40	**5.00**	1.20	.50	2.90	**2.90**	.80	.35	.90	**.90**	.40	.25		
90.00	14.10	**12.30**	2.70	.95	11.00	**10.00**	2.20	.80	8.30	**7.70**	1.60	.65	5.70	**5.40**	1.20	.50	3.20	**3.20**	.90	.35	1.20	**1.20**	.50	.25	.30	.15
91.00	14.10	**12.30**	2.70	.95	11.00	**10.00**	2.20	.80	8.30	**7.70**	1.60	.65	5.70	**5.40**	1.20	.50	3.20	**3.20**	.90	.35	1.20	**1.20**	.50	.25		
92.00	14.50	**12.60**	2.70	1.00	11.40	**10.30**	2.20	.85	8.70	**8.00**	1.70	.70	6.10	**5.70**	1.30	.55	3.50	**3.50**	.90	.40	1.40	**1.40**	.50	.30		
93.00	14.50	**12.60**	2.70	1.00	11.40	**10.30**	2.20	.85	8.70	**8.00**	1.70	.70	6.10	**5.70**	1.30	.55	3.50	**3.50**	.90	.40	1.40	**1.40**	.50	.30		
94.00	14.90	**12.90**	2.80	1.00	11.90	**10.60**	2.30	.85	9.00	**8.30**	1.80	.70	6.40	**6.00**	1.40	.55	3.90	**3.70**	1.00	.40	1.70	**1.70**	.60	.30		
95.00	14.90	**12.90**	2.80	1.00	11.90	**10.60**	2.30	.85	9.00	**8.30**	1.80	.70	6.40	**6.00**	1.40	.55	3.90	**3.70**	1.00	.40	1.70	**1.70**	.60	.30	.30	.15
96.00	15.30	**13.30**	2.90	1.10	12.30	**10.90**	2.40	.90	9.40	**8.60**	1.90	.75	6.80	**6.30**	1.40	.60	4.20	**4.00**	1.00	.45	2.00	**2.00**	.70	.35		.15
97.00	15.30	**13.30**	2.90	1.10	12.30	**10.90**	2.40	.90	9.40	**8.60**	1.90	.75	6.80	**6.30**	1.40	.60	4.20	**4.00**	1.00	.45	2.00	**2.00**	.70	.35		.20
98.00	15.70	**13.60**	3.00	1.10	12.70	**11.30**	2.50	.90	9.80	**9.00**	2.00	.75	7.20	**6.60**	1.50	.60	4.60	**4.30**	1.10	.45	2.30	**2.30**	.70	.35		.20
99.00	15.70	**13.60**	3.00	1.10	12.70	**11.30**	2.50	.90	9.80	**9.00**	2.00	.75	7.20	**6.60**	1.50	.60	4.60	**4.30**	1.10	.45	2.30	**2.30**	.70	.35		.20
100.00	16.50	**14.10**	3.10	1.20	13.40	**11.80**	2.60	1.00	10.40	**9.50**	2.10	.85	7.80	**7.20**	1.60	.70	5.20	**4.90**	1.20	.55	2.80	**2.80**	.80	.40	.30	.20
101.00				1.20				1.00				.85				.70				.55				.40		
102.00				1.20				1.00				.85				.70				.55				.40		
103.00				1.20				1.00				.85				.70				.55				.40		
104.00				1.20				1.00				.85				.70				.55				.40		
105.00	17.50	**14.90**	3.40	1.20	14.50	**12.60**	2.80	1.00	11.50	**10.30**	2.30	.85	8.70	**8.00**	1.80	.70	6.10	**5.70**	1.40	.55	3.50	**3.50**	1.00	.40	.30	.20
106.00																										.20
107.00																										.20
108.00																										.25
109.00																										.25
110.00	18.60	**15.70**	3.60	1.30	15.50	**13.40**	3.00	1.15	12.50	**11.10**	2.50	1.00	9.60	**8.80**	2.00	.85	7.00	**6.50**	1.50	.65	4.40	**4.20**	1.10	.50	.30	.25
111.00																										
112.00																										
113.00																										
114.00																										
115.00	19.60	**16.50**	3.90	1.30	16.60	**14.20**	3.30	1.15	13.60	**11.90**	2.70	1.00	10.50	**9.60**	2.20	.85	7.90	**7.30**	1.70	.65	5.30	**5.00**	1.30	.50	.30	.25
116.00																										.25
117.00																										.25
118.00																										.25
119.00																										.30
120.00	20.70	**17.30**	4.20	1.50	17.60	**15.00**	3.50	1.30	14.60	**12.70**	2.90	1.15	11.60	**10.40**	2.40	.95	8.80	**8.10**	1.90	.80	6.20	**5.80**	1.40	.65	.30	.30
121.00																										
122.00																										
123.00																										
124.00																										
125.00	21.70	**18.10**	4.40	1.50	18.70	**15.80**	3.80	1.30	15.70	**13.50**	3.10	1.15	12.60	**11.20**	2.60	.95	9.70	**8.90**	2.10	.80	7.10	**6.60**	1.60	.65	.30	.30
126.00																										
127.00																										
128.00																										
129.00																										
130.00	22.80	**18.90**	4.70	1.65	19.70	**16.60**	4.00	1.45	16.70	**14.30**	3.40	1.30	13.70	**12.00**	2.80	1.10	10.70	**9.70**	2.30	.95	8.00	**7.40**	1.80	.80	.30	.35
131.00																										
132.00																										
133.00																										
134.00																										
135.00	23.80	**19.70**	4.90	1.65	20.80	**17.40**	4.30	1.45	17.80	**15.10**	3.60	1.30	14.70	**12.80**	3.00	1.10	11.70	**10.50**	2.50	.95	8.90	**8.20**	2.00	.80	.30	.35
136.00																										
137.00																										
138.00																										
139.00																										

a) The New York State withholding tax for a person with one allowance who earned $85.00 is $1.90; the New York City tax on this resident is $.75.

b) The social security tax is $4.97; the federal withholding tax is $9.80.

Problems

1. Tom earned $90.00 last week. He is single and claimed one allowance. How much should be taken out of his pay for:
   a) State withholding tax?
   b) City withholding tax?

2. Mr. Zamore earned $94.00. He is married, and claimed 2 allowances. How much should be taken out of his pay for:
   a) State withholding tax?
   b) City withholding tax?

3. For each of the following employees, find the social security tax, the federal withholding tax, the New York State withholding tax, the N.Y.C. withholding tax, and the take-home pay.

Name	Weekly Wage	Single or Married	Number of Allowances
a) Mr. Monroe	$88.00	Single	1
b) Mr. Nanes	92.00	Married	2
c) Mr. Oppenheimer	85.25	Single	2
d) Mr. Parks	85.50	Married	2
e) Mr. Queens	85.60	Married	3
f) Mr. Rosen	85.75	Married	2
g) Mr. Stern	93.05	Single	2

SECTION 9 New York State Disability Benefits

Class Drill

1. Find 1% of $50
2. Find 1% of $36
3. Find 1% of $60
4. Find 1% of $45

5. Find ½% of $30
6. Find ½% of $46
7. Find ½% of $60
8. Find ½% of $58

Sample Problem

Joe earns $85 a week. How much will be taken out of his pay for New York State disability benefits?

Explanation

In New York State, a worker receives cash benefits when he is disabled by an OFF-THE-JOB injury or illness. (The Workman's Compensation Law provides cash benefits and medical care for a worker injured on the job.)

Cash benefits are 50% of average weekly wages with a maximum benefit of $75 per week. Benefits are payable for a maximum of 26 weeks of disability during 52 consecutive weeks. No benefits are paid during the first seven days of disability.

The employer deducts ½ of 1% of the first $60 of weekly wages, but no more than 30¢ a week.

Sample Solution

Since Joe earned more than $60, the disability benefits deduction of 30¢ will be taken out of his pay.

1% of $60 is $.60
½ of $.60 is $.30

Problems

1. Mr. Green earned $50 last week. How much will be taken out of his pay for disability benefits?

2. Mr. Thompson earned $55 last week. What will be taken out of his pay for disability benefits?

3. For each of the following employees, find the amount that would be deducted for disability benefits.

Name	Wage
a) Mr. Stevens	$44
b) Mr. Torme	56
c) Mr. Van Dam	59
d) Mr. West	56.20
e) Mr. Young	75
f) Mr. Zeller	57.80

SECTION 10   Use of Payroll Form; Currency Distribution

Class Drill

Add:
1. $ 4.75 + $5.45 + $6.32
2. $16.75 + $5.50 + $ .70
3. $18.19 + $4.33 + $1.50
4. $17.42 + $8.59 + $ .60

Subtract:
5. $143.15 – $23.50
6. $121.89 – $17.43
7. $ 95.43 – $ 8.79
8. $101.52 – $ 6.41

Sample Problem

Mr. Stevens earned $90 last week. He is single and claimed one exemption.
a) Find his take-home pay.
b) Prepare the currency distribution.

Some firms use checks in order to pay employees; some put cash in pay envelopes. When envelopes are used, it is necessary to decide on the exact bills and coins needed, in advance, so that the correct denominations may be obtained at the bank. A form is used known as a currency distribution form.

When a firm finds the take-home pay for many employees, the work is shown on a special payroll form. Your teacher will provide these forms when they are needed, and will also provide currency distribution forms. Samples of these forms are shown on the next page.

Sample Solution

a)

Salary	S.S. Tax	Fed. W.T.	State W.T.	City W.T.	Dis. Tax	Total Ded.	Net Pay
$90.00	5.27	11.00	2.20	.80	.30	19.57	$70.43

b)

Employee	Net Pay	$10	$5	$1	$.50	$.25	$.10	$.05	$.01
J. Stevens	$70.43	7				1	1	1	3

Problems

1. Prepare the payroll for the following employees for the week ending February 7, and then prepare the currency distribution. Use forms provided by your teacher. Show totals for the week.

Employee	Status	Allowances	Earnings
Mr. Adams	S	1	$80.00
Mr. Brown	M	2	85.00
Mr. Charles	M	3	90.00

2. Prepare the payroll and currency distribution for the three men in example 1 for the week ending February 14. Earnings are shown below. There was no change in status or allowances. Show totals for the week.

Mr. Adams	$82.00
Mr. Brown	88.00
Mr. Charles	91.00

3. Prepare the payroll and the currency distribution, as above, for the week ending February 21:

Mr. Adams	$83.25
Mr. Brown	89.50
Mr. Charles	92.75

4. Prepare the payroll and currency distribution, as above, for the week ending February 28:

Mr. Adams	$81.40
Mr. Brown	87.65
Mr. Charles	93.15

5. (Optional) Prepare the payroll for the following employees for the week ending March 7. Allow time and one-half for overtime.

Employee	Status	Allowances	M T W Th F Hours Worked	Hourly Rate
Mr. Miller	S	1	8 8 8 8 8	$2.00
Mr. Natcher	M	3	8 8 8 8 8	2.25
Mr. Olson	M	2	8 9 8 9 8	2.10

PAYROLL FOR THE WEEK ENDED *February 9, 1973*

CARD NO.	EMPLOYEE	STATUS	EXEM.	M	T	W	TH	F	S	REG.	O.T.	HOURLY RATE	REGULAR	OVERTIME	TOTAL	FICA TAX	FED. WITH. TAX	N.Y. STATE WITH. TAX	N.Y. CITY WITH. TAX	DIS. BEN.			TOTAL DED.	NET PAY
25	J. Stevens	S	1	8	8	8	8	8		40		2 25	90 00		90 00	5 27	11 00	2 20	80	30			19 57	70 43
26	W. Thompson	S	1	8	8	8	8	8		40		2 00	80 00		80 00	4 68	9 10	1 70	70	30			16 48	63 52
27	B. Walters	M	2	8	8	10	8	8		40	2	2 00	80 00	6 00	86 00	5 03	7 00	1 50	60	30			14 43	71 57
													250 00	6 00	256 00	14 98	27 10	5 40	2 10	90			50 48	205 52

| | | | | | | | | | | | | | | | | | | | | | | | | |

CURRENCY DISTRIBUTION

PAYROLL FOR THE WEEK ENDING *February 9, 1973*

Employee	Net Wages		Bills			Coins			
		$10	$5	$1	$.50	$.25	$.10	$.05	$.01
J. Stevens	70	43	7				1	1	1	3
W. Thompson	63	52	6		3	1				2
B. Walters	71	57	7		1	1			1	2
	205	52	20		4	2	1	1	2	7

SECTION 11   Review Problems

1. Shown below are two time cards of employees of the Empire Supply Co. In this firm any lateness up to 15 minutes costs the worker 15 minutes pay; any lateness from 16 minutes to 30 minutes costs the worker 30 minutes pay, etc. Workers in this firm are supposed to work from 8 A.M. to 12:00 Noon, and from 1 P.M. to 5 P.M.

Mr. Jordan Rate per hour: $3.00					Mr. Kennedy Rate per hour: $4.00			
	In	Out	In	Out		In	Out	In	Out
M	7:59	12:01	12:55	5:01	M	8:00	12:10	12:58	5:01
T	8:00	12:02	1:05	5:05	T	7:55	12:03	12:56	5:06
W	8:10	12:00	1:00	5:00	W	8:07	12:01	12:59	5:04
Th	7:54	12:06	12:59	5:02	Th	8:19	12:02	12:58	5:02
F	8:12	12:03	12:57	5:05	F	8:23	12:01	1:08	5:01

For each worker, find: a. the number of hours worked daily and for the week

b. the amount earned for the week

2. The following information was obtained from the time cards:

	Hours Worked					Rate per Hour
	M	T	W	Th	F	
Mr. C.	8	8	8	8	8	$2.75
Mr. D.	$7\frac{1}{2}$	8	$7\frac{1}{2}$	8	8	2.80
Mr. E	$7\frac{1}{2}$	$7\frac{1}{4}$	$7\frac{1}{2}$	8	8	3.00

   a. How many hours did each work during the week?
   b. How much did each earn for the week?

3. Bill worked 44 hours during the week. If he earns time and one-half for overtime, and his regular week consists of 40 hours, find his earnings if he makes $2.80 an hour.

4. Harry worked 47 hours during the week. He earns $3.00 an hour, time and one-half for overtime. How much did he earn?

5. Mr. Lester earns $6,500 a year.
   a. How much does he earn a month? (to the nearest cent)
   b. How much does he earn a week?

6. Mr. Nadler receives a salary of $45 a week plus a commission of 30% on sales. If he sold $310 worth of merchandise during the week, how much did he earn?

7. Sally earns $75 a week.
   a. Without using the table, find her deduction for social security tax.
   b. Use the table to check your answer.

8. George earned $87 last week. He is single and claims one allowance.
   a. Find his take-home pay.
   b. Prepare the form showing the currency needed for his pay.

UNIT 5

Income Taxes

SECTION 1 Federal Income Tax: Income Less Than Filing
Requirement

Class Drill

1. Find 10% of $2,356
2. Find 10% of $3,575
3. Find 10% of $4,657
4. Find 1% of $2,125
5. Find 1% of $1,450

6. Subtract $150.25 from $357.50
7. Subtract $127.83 from $243.21
8. Subtract $235.24 from $611.00
9. Add: $153.13, $248.27, $964.15
10. Add: $175.00, $221.52, $353.89

Sample Problem

Bill, a high school student, worked most of the summer and earned $900.
Each week his employer deducted money from his pay for federal withholding tax. By the end of the summer, he had deducted a total of $83.00.
a) *Must* Bill file a federal income tax return?
b) *Should* Bill file a federal income tax return?
c) If he should file the return, prepare it for him.

Explanation

In the previous topic you learned how the employer prepared the payroll.
When Bill started to work, the employer asked him to fill out Form W-4,
Employee's Withholding Allowance Certificate. (See page 52)

On line (a), Bill claimed an allowance because he is single. Beginning in
1972, Bill could claim a "special withholding allowance" on line (h). This
special allowance may be claimed by a single person who does not have two
or more jobs, and by married people unless both husband and wife are
employed.

Bill could have asked to fill out Form W-4E, "Exemption from Withholding" if he had had no federal income tax liability the previous year and did
not expect to have any last year when he worked during the summer. (See
page 53)

If Bill had signed Form W-4E, his employer would not have taken any federal withholding tax out of his pay. This form was available for the first time April 30, 1970, as part of the Tax Reform Act of 1969. However, Bill had earned a good deal of money the previous year, and had had to pay a federal income tax, so he did not file Form W-4E.

The employer found how much to take out of Bill's salary by looking at the federal withholding tax table, as you learned previously. After the end of the year, the employer computed how much each employee had earned during the year and how much was taken out of his pay for federal withholding tax. The employer then prepared for each employee form W-2, Wage and Tax Statement. Eight copies were distributed as follows: one copy to the Internal Revenue Service; one copy to the State Income Tax Bureau; one copy to the New York City Finance Administration; one copy was kept by the employer, and four copies were given to the employee. The employee should attach one copy to his federal return, one to his state return, one to his city return, and should keep one copy for his own records.

Bills W-2 statement appeared as follows:

WAGE AND TAX STATEMENT 1972

(For use in States or Cities authorizing combined form)

Employer's State Identification Number

Copy B—To be filed with employee's FEDERAL tax return

Type or print EMPLOYER'S Federal Identification number, name, and address above.

FEDERAL INCOME TAX INFORMATION			SOCIAL SECURITY INFORMATION		STATUS	*
Federal income tax withheld	Wages paid subject to withholding in 1972 [1]	Other compensation paid in 1972 [2]	FICA employee tax withheld [3]	Total FICA wages paid in 1972 [4]	1. Single 2. Married	
$83.00	$900.00		$46.80		S	**

EMPLOYEE'S social security number ▶ 096-54-6372

WILLIAM JONES
712 41 Street
Woodside, New York 11177

Name of State	State Form No.	State income tax withheld
N. Y.	IT 2102	22 ¦ 00

Name of City	City Form No.	City income tax withheld
N. Y.	NYC-2	7 ¦ 00

*Excludable sick pay. **Gross wages for State if different from Federal.
[1] Includes tips reported by employee. Amount is before payroll deductions or sick pay exclusion.
[2] Add this item to wages in reporting wages and salaries on your income tax return.
[3] The social security (FICA) rate of 5.2% includes .6% for Hospital Insurance Benefits and 4.6% for old-age, survivors, and disability insurance.
[4] Includes tips reported by employee.

Type or print EMPLOYEE'S name and address (including ZIP code) above.

Uncollected Employee Tax on Tips . . . $

FORM W-2 Department of the Treasury, Internal Revenue Service

Who Must File a Tax Return?

The tax law requires that every individual who had more than a certain amount of income for the year must file a federal income tax return. Before 1970, any individual earning $600 or more during the year had to file a tax return. During the past few years this amount has gradually been increased. Starting in 1973, a tax return must be filed if a single person had income of at least $2,050, or a married couple had income of $2,800. There is one exception, however. If a single person could be claimed as a dependent on his parent's tax return, and he has unearned income, such as interest income or dividend income, then he must file a tax return if his income was $750 or more.

Inasmuch as Bill had no unearned income such as interest income, and he earned less than $2,050 during the year, he is not required to file a tax return, and he does not have to pay any income tax. However, in order to obtain a refund of the $83.00 that was taken out of his pay, Bill has to file a tax return.

Which Tax Return Should Be Filed?

There are two types of tax returns: Short Form 1040A, and Form 1040. The Short Form may be used when income was from wages and not more than $200 in interest income or $200 in dividend income, and the person does not wish to list his deductions. Most students should be able to use Short From 1040A.

Meaning of Exemption

Bill is entitled to one exemption for himself. The "special withholding allowance" shown on the W-4 form for a single person who has only one job applies only to the withholding tax, and does not apply to the tax return. Bill could have two allowances, but only one exemption.

When Must the Tax Return Be Filed?

The tax return must be filed by April 15 each year, to report income received during the previous year.

Sample Solution

a) Bill is not required to file a tax return.
b) Bill should file a tax return to obtain a refund of the federal withholding tax that was deducted from his pay.
c) The completed tax return is shown on page 66. The front of Short Form 1040A is shown at the top, and the back of the form is shown at the bottom.

Problems

1. John earned $1200 in wages last year. He had no other income. He filed Form W-4E with his employer.
   a) *Must* he file a tax return? Explain.
   b) *Should* he file a tax return? Explain.

2. Sam earned $700 last year. He filed Form W-4E with his employer.
   a) *Must* he file a tax return? Explain.
   b) *Should* he file a tax return? Explain.

3. Assume you earned $625 last year, and that $50 was deducted from your pay for federal withholding tax. (You filed Form W-4)
   a) Why should you file a federal income tax return?
   b) Prepare the return. (Use Short Form 1040A. Use your own name, address and social security number. Your teacher will provide the form to use. She may ask you to use the form in Publication 21, "Understanding Taxes" prepared by the Internal Revenue Service, or she may give you an actual Form 1040A or a mimeographed copy of it.)

FORM 1040A – Front

Short Form 1040A   **U.S. Individual Income Tax Return**   Department of the Treasury Internal Revenue Service **1972**

Please print or type

First name and initial (if joint return, use first names and middle initials of both) **WILLIAM**   Last name **JONES**

Your social security number (Husband's, if joint return) **096 54 6372**

Present home address (Number and street (including apartment number) or rural route) **712 41 St.**

Wife's number, if joint return

City, town or post office, State and ZIP code **WOODSIDE, N.Y. 11177**

Occupation Yours **CLERK**   Wife's

Filing Status—check only one:

1 ☑ Single
2 ☐ Married filing joint return
3 ☐ Married filing separately. If wife (husband) is also filing, give her (his) social security number and first name here.

4 ☐ Unmarried Head of Household
5 ☐ Widow(er) with dependent child (Enter year of death of husband (wife) ► 19   )

Exemptions

	Regular	65 or over	Blind	Enter number of boxes checked ►
6 Yourself . . .	☑	☐	☐	**1**
7 Wife (husband) .	☐	☐	☐	

8 First names of your dependent children *who lived with you*

Enter number ►

9 Number of other dependents (from line 25) . . . . ►
10 Total exemptions claimed . . . . ► **1**

11	Wages, salaries, tips, etc. (attach Form W-2 to front. If unavailable, attach explanation)	11	**900 00**
12a	Dividends (if over $200, use Form 1040—see instructions)$.............. 12b Less Exclusion $.............. **Balance ►**	12c	
13	Interest income (if over $200, use Form 1040)	13	
14	Total lines 11, 12c, and 13 (Adjusted Gross Income)	14	**900 00**

- If line 14 is $20,000 or less and you want IRS to figure your tax, see instructions on page 3.
- If line 14 is under $10,000, find tax in Tables 1–12 and enter on line 19. Skip lines 15 through 18.
- If line 14 is $10,000 or more go to line 15.

15	If line 14 is $10,000 or more, enter 15% of line 14 but not more than $2,000 ($1,000 if line 3 was checked) .	15	
16	Subtract line 15 from line 14	16	
17	Multiply total number of exemptions claimed on line 10 by $750	17	
18	Taxable income (subtract line 17 from line 16)	18	

(Figure tax on amount on line 18 using Tax Rate Schedule X, Y, or Z, and enter tax on line 19.)

Attach Copy B of Form W-2 here
Attach Check or Money Order here

FORM 1040A – Back

Form 1040A (1972)   Page **2**

19	Tax, check if from: ☑ Tax Tables 1–12, or ☐ Tax Rate Schedule X, Y, or Z . .	19	**0 00**
20	Credit for contributions to candidates for public office (see instructions on page 5)	20	**0 00**
21	Income tax (subtract line 20 from line 19). If less than zero, enter zero	21	**0 00**
22	Total Federal income tax withheld (attach Form W-2 to front)	22	**83 00**
23	If line 21 is larger than line 22, enter BALANCE DUE IRS. Pay in full with return. Write social security number on check or money order and make payable to Internal Revenue Service ►	23	
24	If line 22 is larger than line 21, enter REFUND. . . . . ►	24	**83 00**

Other Dependents

(a) NAME	(b) Relationship	(c) Months lived in your home. If born or died during year, write B or D.	(d) Did dependent have income of $750 or more?	(e) Amount YOU furnished for dependent's support. If 100% write ALL.	(f) Amount furnished by OTHERS including dependent.
				$	$

25 Total number of dependents listed in column (a). Enter here and on line 9 . . . . ►

Revenue Sharing

26 Print or type the location of your principal place of residence at end of year (not necessarily the same as your post office address).

(a) State	(b) County	(c) Locality. If you lived inside the boundaries of an incorporated city, town, etc., enter its name; if not, check here . . . ► ☐	(d) Township (see instructions on page 5)
NY	QUEENS	NEW YORK CITY	

27 Enter the number of persons included on line 10 who (1) are filing a return of their own; or, (2) did not live at your principal place of residence at the end of the year . . . . ►

For IRS use only—Leave blank

Under penalties of perjury, I declare that I have examined this return, including accompanying schedules and statements, and to the best of my knowledge and belief it is true, correct, and complete. Declaration of preparer (other than taxpayer) is based on all information of which he has any knowledge.

Sign here ► *William Jones*   3/1/73
Your signature   Date

► Preparer's signature (other than taxpayer)   Date

► Wife's (husband's) signature (if filing jointly, BOTH must sign even if only one had income)   Address (and ZIP Code)   Preparer's Emp. Ident. or Soc. Sec. No.

☆☆☆☆ U.S. GOVERNMENT PRINTING OFFICE:1972—O-458-274   E. I. No. 23-1328538

66

4. Assume you earned $990 last year, all from wages and that $98 was deducted from your pay for federal withholding tax. (You filed Form W-4)
   a) Why should you file a federal income tax return?
   b) Prepare the return. Use Short Form 1040A.

5. (Optional) Bill now earns $45 a week. He is single, and filed Form W-4 with his employer. Bill claimed 1 allowance for himself plus 1 special withholding allowance.
   a) Consult current federal withholding tax tables to find the amount of federal withholding tax taken out of his pay each week.
   b) If he works 30 weeks this year, how much should the W-2 form show as "Wages Paid" for the year?
   c) If he works 30 weeks this year, how much should the W-2 form show as "Federal Income Tax Withheld" for the year?
   d) When he prepares his Form 1040A, how much should he ask as his refund?

6. (Optional) Assume Tom earns $35 a week working part time, and is single. He filed Form W-4 with his employer. Answer questions a, b, c, d, shown in problem 5. Tom claimed 1 allowance for himself and 1 special withholding allowance.

SECTION 2

Federal Income Tax: Income Less Than $10,000; Use of Tax Table

Class Drill

Multiply:

1. $4.20 × 52	4. $52 × 10
2. $5.30 × 52	5. $47 × 12
3. $6.25 × 52	6. $53 × 13

Sample Problem

According to his W-2 form, George, who is single, earned $4,160 last year, and $338 was deducted from his pay for federal withholding tax. George also had some money in a savings bank, and earned $50 interest on it during the year.
   a) Must George file a federal income tax return? Why?
   b) Prepare the return.

Explanation

We learned previously that a single person must file a federal tax return if his income was $2,050 or more.

If the income was less than $10,000, the person may find his tax from a table prepared by the Internal Revenue Service. There is a table for a person with one exemption, another table for a person with two exemptions, etc. The table for a person with one exemption is shown on page 68.

The term "income" includes income received from wages, from interest, from dividends, from tips, etc.

For persons with incomes under $10,000 using Short Form 1040A.

1972 Tax Tables

The standard deduction and deduction for exemptions have been taken into account in determining the tax shown in these Tables.

The Tables show the lower tax after taking into account both the percentage standard deduction and the low income allowance except in the case of married persons filing separately. For married persons filing separate returns, the tables show the tax figured on the percentage standard deduction and on the low income allowance.

Select the Tax Table that covers the total number of exemptions on Short Form 1040A, line 10. On the appropriate table, read down the income columns until you find the line covering the income you entered on Short Form 1040A, line 14. Then read across to the column heading describing your filing status. If you checked line 5, use the column for "Married filing joint return." Enter the tax you find there on Short Form 1040A, line 19.

Married persons filing separate returns: Choose either the low income allowance or percentage standard deduction to figure your tax; but if one uses the percentage standard deduction, then both must use it. If you are a married person living apart from your spouse, see paragraph 1(d), page 6 of the instructions in this package to see if you can be considered to be "unmarried" for purposes of using the tax tables below.

Table 1 —Returns claiming ONE exemption (and not itemizing deductions)

If the amount on Form 1040A, line 14, is— At least	But less than	Single, not head of household	Head of household	Married filing separate return claiming— Low income allowance	Married filing separate return claiming— %Standard deduction
$0	$875	$0	$0	$0	$0
875	900	0	0	0	1
900	925	0	0	0	4
925	950	0	0	0	7
950	975	0	0	0	10
975	1,000	0	0	0	13
1,000	1,025	0	0	0	15
1,025	1,050	0	0	0	18
1,050	1,075	0	0	0	21
1,075	1,100	0	0	0	24
1,100	1,125	0	0	0	27
1,125	1,150	0	0	0	30
1,150	1,175	0	0	0	33
1,175	1,200	0	0	0	36
1,200	1,225	0	0	0	39
1,225	1,250	0	0	0	42
1,250	1,275	0	0	0	45
1,275	1,300	0	0	0	48
1,300	1,325	0	0	0	51
1,325	1,350	0	0	0	54
1,350	1,375	0	0	0	57
1,375	1,400	0	0	0	60
1,400	1,425	0	0	2	63
1,425	1,450	0	0	5	66
1,450	1,475	0	0	9	69
1,475	1,500	0	0	12	72
1,500	1,525	0	0	16	75
1,525	1,550	0	0	19	79
1,550	1,575	0	0	23	82
1,575	1,600	0	0	26	85
1,600	1,625	0	0	30	88
1,625	1,650	0	0	33	91
1,650	1,675	0	0	37	94
1,675	1,700	0	0	40	98
1,700	1,725	0	0	44	101
1,725	1,750	0	0	47	104
1,750	1,775	0	0	51	107
1,775	1,800	0	0	54	110
1,800	1,825	0	0	58	114
1,825	1,850	0	0	61	117
1,850	1,875	0	0	65	120
1,875	1,900	0	0	68	123
1,900	1,925	0	0	72	126
1,925	1,950	0	0	76	130
1,950	1,975	0	0	79	133
1,975	2,000	0	0	83	136
2,000	2,025	0	0	87	139
2,025	2,050	0	0	91	142
2,050	2,075	2	2	94	145
2,075	2,100	5	5	98	149
2,100	2,125	9	9	102	152
2,125	2,150	12	12	106	156
2,150	2,175	16	16	109	159
2,175	2,200	19	19	113	162
2,200	2,225	23	23	117	166
2,225	2,250	26	26	121	169
2,250	2,275	30	30	124	173
2,275	2,300	33	33	128	176
2,300	2,325	37	37	132	179
2,325	2,350	40	40	136	183
2,350	2,375	44	44	139	186
2,375	2,400	47	47	143	190
2,400	2,425	51	51	147	193
2,425	2,450	54	54	151	196
2,450	2,475	58	58	155	200
2,475	2,500	61	61	159	203
2,500	2,525	65	65	163	207
2,525	2,550	68	68	167	210
2,550	2,575	72	72	171	213
2,575	2,600	76	75	175	217
2,600	2,625	79	79	179	220
2,625	2,650	83	82	183	224
2,650	2,675	87	86	187	227
2,675	2,700	91	89	191	231
2,700	2,725	94	93	195	234
2,725	2,750	98	96	199	238
2,750	2,775	102	100	203	242
2,775	2,800	106	103	207	245
2,800	2,825	109	107	211	249
2,825	2,850	113	110	215	253
2,850	2,875	117	114	219	256
2,875	2,900	121	117	223	260
2,900	2,925	124	121	227	263
2,925	2,950	128	124	231	267
2,950	2,975	132	128	236	271
2,975	3,000	136	131	240	274
3,000	3,050	141	137	246	280
3,050	3,100	149	144	255	287
3,100	3,150	157	152	263	294
3,150	3,200	165	160	272	301
3,200	3,250	173	168	280	309
3,250	3,300	181	176	289	316
3,300	3,350	189	184	297	324
3,350	3,400	197	192	306	333
3,400	3,450	205	200	315	341
3,450	3,500	213	208	324	349
3,500	3,550	221	216	334	357
3,550	3,600	229	224	343	365
3,600	3,650	238	232	353	373
3,650	3,700	246	240	362	381
3,700	3,750	255	248	372	389
3,750	3,800	263	256	381	397
3,800	3,850	272	264	391	406
3,850	3,900	280	272	400	413
3,900	3,950	289	280	410	421
3,950	4,000	297	288	419	429
4,000	4,050	306	296	429	438
4,050	4,100	315	305	438	446
4,100	4,150	324	314	448	454
4,150	4,200	334	323	457	462
4,200	4,250	343	332	467	470
4,250	4,300	353	341	476	478
4,300	4,350	362	350	486	486
4,350	4,400	372	359	495	494
4,400	4,450	381	368	505	502
4,450	4,500	391	377	514	510
4,500	4,550	400	386	524	518
4,550	4,600	410	395	533	526
4,600	4,650	419	404	543	534
4,650	4,700	429	413	552	543
4,700	4,750	438	422	562	551
4,750	4,800	448	431	571	559
4,800	4,850	457	440	581	567
4,850	4,900	467	449	590	575
4,900	4,950	476	458	600	583
4,950	5,000	486	467	609	591
5,000	5,050	495	476	619	599
5,050	5,100	505	485	628	607
5,100	5,150	514	494	638	615
5,150	5,200	524	503	647	623
5,200	5,250	533	512	657	631
5,250	5,300	543	521	666	639
5,300	5,350	552	530	676	647
5,350	5,400	562	539	685	656
5,400	5,450	571	548	696	664
5,450	5,500	581	557	707	672
5,500	5,550	590	566	718	680
5,550	5,600	600	575	729	688
5,600	5,650	609	584	740	697
5,650	5,700	619	593	751	706
5,700	5,750	628	602	762	716
5,750	5,800	638	611	773	725
5,800	5,850	647	620	784	734
5,850	5,900	657	629	795	744
5,900	5,950	666	638	806	753
5,950	6,000	676	647	817	762
6,000	6,050	685	656	828	772
6,050	6,100	695	665	839	781
6,100	6,150	706	674	850	790
6,150	6,200	716	684	861	800
6,200	6,250	727	693	872	809
6,250	6,300	737	703	883	818
6,300	6,350	748	712	894	828
6,350	6,400	758	722	905	837
6,400	6,450	769	731	916	846
6,450	6,500	779	741	927	856
6,500	6,550	790	750	938	865
6,550	6,600	800	760	949	875
6,600	6,650	811	769	960	884
6,650	6,700	821	779	971	894
6,700	6,750	832	788	982	905
6,750	6,800	842	798	993	916
6,800	6,850	853	807	1,004	927
6,850	6,900	863	817	1,015	938
6,900	6,950	874	826	1,026	949
6,950	7,000	884	836	1,037	960
7,000	7,050	895	845	1,048	971
7,050	7,100	905	855	1,059	982
7,100	7,150	916	864	1,070	993
7,150	7,200	926	874	1,081	1,004
7,200	7,250	937	883	1,092	1,015
7,250	7,300	947	893	1,103	1,026
7,300	7,350	958	902	1,114	1,037
7,350	7,400	968	912	1,125	1,048
7,400	7,450	979	921	1,136	1,059
7,450	7,500	989	931	1,149	1,070
7,500	7,550	1,000	940	1,161	1,081
7,550	7,600	1,010	950	1,174	1,092
7,600	7,650	1,021	959	1,186	1,103
7,650	7,700	1,031	969	1,199	1,114
7,700	7,750	1,042	978	1,211	1,125
7,750	7,800	1,052	988	1,224	1,136
7,800	7,850	1,063	997	1,236	1,149
7,850	7,900	1,073	1,007	1,249	1,161
7,900	7,950	1,084	1,016	1,261	1,174
7,950	8,000	1,094	1,026	1,274	1,186
8,000	8,050	1,105	1,035	1,286	1,199
8,050	8,100	1,116	1,046	1,299	1,211
8,100	8,150	1,128	1,057	1,311	1,224
8,150	8,200	1,140	1,068	1,324	1,236
8,200	8,250	1,152	1,079	1,336	1,249
8,250	8,300	1,164	1,090	1,349	1,261
8,300	8,350	1,176	1,101	1,361	1,274
8,350	8,400	1,188	1,112	1,374	1,286
8,400	8,450	1,200	1,123	1,386	1,299
8,450	8,500	1,212	1,134	1,399	1,311
8,500	8,550	1,224	1,145	1,411	1,324
8,550	8,600	1,236	1,156	1,424	1,336
8,600	8,650	1,248	1,167	1,436	1,349
8,650	8,700	1,260	1,177	1,449	1,361
8,700	8,750	1,270	1,187	1,461	1,374
8,750	8,800	1,280	1,196	1,474	1,386
8,800	8,850	1,290	1,205	1,486	1,399
8,850	8,900	1,301	1,215	1,499	1,411
8,900	8,950	1,311	1,224	1,511	1,424
8,950	9,000	1,321	1,233	1,524	1,436
9,000	9,050	1,331	1,243	1,536	1,449
9,050	9,100	1,341	1,252	1,549	1,461
9,100	9,150	1,352	1,261	1,561	1,474
9,150	9,200	1,362	1,271	1,574	1,486
9,200	9,250	1,372	1,280	1,586	1,499
9,250	9,300	1,382	1,289	1,599	1,511
9,300	9,350	1,392	1,299	1,611	1,524
9,350	9,400	1,403	1,308	1,624	1,536
9,400	9,450	1,413	1,317	1,637	1,549
9,450	9,500	1,423	1,327	1,651	1,561
9,500	9,550	1,433	1,336	1,665	1,574
9,550	9,600	1,443	1,346	1,679	1,587
9,600	9,650	1,454	1,355	1,693	1,599
9,650	9,700	1,464	1,364	1,707	1,611
9,700	9,750	1,474	1,374	1,721	1,624
9,750	9,800	1,484	1,383	1,735	1,637
9,800	9,850	1,494	1,392	1,749	1,651
9,850	9,900	1,505	1,402	1,763	1,665
9,900	9,950	1,515	1,411	1,777	1,679
9,950	10,000	1,525	1,420	1,791	1,693

FORM 1040A — Front

Short Form 1040A   **U.S. Individual Income Tax Return**   Department of the Treasury Internal Revenue Service   **1972**

Please print or type

First name and initial (if joint return, use first names and middle initials of both): **GEORGE**   Last name: **BAKER**

Your social security number (Husband's, if joint return): **214 63 1018**

Present home address (Number and street (including apartment number) or rural route): **7510 32 AVE.**

Wife's number, if joint return

City, town or post office, State and ZIP code: **LONG ISLAND CITY, N.Y. 11103**

Occupation — Yours: **CLERK**   Wife's:

Filing Status—check only one:
1. ☑ Single
2. ☐ Married filing joint return
3. ☐ Married filing separately. If wife (husband) is also filing, give her (his) social security number and first name here.
4. ☐ Unmarried Head of Household
5. ☐ Widow(er) with dependent child (Enter year of death of husband (wife) ► 19   )

Exemptions   Regular   65 or over   Blind   Enter number of boxes checked ► **1**
6. Yourself . . . ☑ ☐ ☐
7. Wife (husband) . . ☐ ☐ ☐
8. First names of your dependent children who lived with you

    Enter number ►

9. Number of other dependents (from line 25) . . . . ►
10. Total exemptions claimed . . . . ► **1**

Attach Copy B of Form W–2 here / Attach Check or Money Order here

11	Wages, salaries, tips, etc. (attach Form W–2 to front. If unavailable, attach explanation)	11	4160 00
12a	Dividends (if over $200, use Form 1040—see instructions)$.................... 12b Less Exclusion $.................... Balance ►	12c	
13	Interest income (if over $200, use Form 1040)	13	50 00
14	Total lines 11, 12c, and 13 (Adjusted Gross Income)	14	4210 00

● If line 14 is $20,000 or less and you want IRS to figure your tax, see instructions on page 3.
● If line 14 is under $10,000, find tax in Tables 1–12 and enter on line 19. Skip lines 15 through 18.
● If line 14 is $10,000 or more go to line 15.

15	If line 14 is $10,000 or more, enter 15% of line 14 but not more than $2,000 ($1,000 if line 3 was checked) .	15	
16	Subtract line 15 from line 14	16	
17	Multiply total number of exemptions claimed on line 10 by $750	17	
18	Taxable income (subtract line 17 from line 16)	18	

(Figure tax on amount on line 18 using Tax Rate Schedule X, Y, or Z, and enter tax on line 19.)

FORM 1040A — Back

Form 1040A (1972)   Page **2**

19	Tax, check if from: ☑ Tax Tables 1–12, or ☐ Tax Rate Schedule X, Y, or Z . .	19	343 00
20	Credit for contributions to candidates for public office (see instructions on page 5)	20	0 00
21	Income tax (subtract line 20 from line 19). If less than zero, enter zero	21	343 00
22	Total Federal income tax withheld (attach Form W–2 to front)	22	338 00
23	If line 21 is larger than line 22, enter BALANCE DUE IRS. Pay in full with return. Write social security number on check or money order and make payable to Internal Revenue Service ►	23	5 00
24	If line 22 is larger than line 21, enter REFUND. . . . . ►	24	

Other Dependents

(a) NAME	(b) Relationship	(c) Months lived in your home. If born or died during year, write B or D.	(d) Did dependent have income of $750 or more?	(e) Amount YOU furnished for dependent's support. If 100% write ALL. $	(f) Amount furnished by OTHERS including dependent. $

25 Total number of dependents listed in column (a). Enter here and on line 9 . . . . ►

Revenue Sharing

26 Print or type the location of your principal place of residence at end of year (not necessarily the same as your post office address).

(a) State	(b) County	(c) Locality. If you lived inside the boundaries of an incorporated city, town, etc., enter its name; if not, check here . . . ► ☐	(d) Township (see instructions on page 5)
NY	QUEENS	NEW YORK CITY	

27 Enter the number of persons included on line 10 who (1) are filing a return of their own; or, (2) did not live at your principal place of residence at the end of the year . . . . . ►

For IRS use only—Leave blank

Under penalties of perjury, I declare that I have examined this return, including accompanying schedules and statements, and to the best of my knowledge and belief it is true, correct, and complete. Declaration of preparer (other than taxpayer) is based on all information of which he has any knowledge.

Sign here
Your signature: *George Baker*   Date: 3/15/73
Preparer's signature (other than taxpayer)   Date
Wife's (husband's) signature (if filing jointly, BOTH must sign even if only one had income)   Address (and ZIP Code)   Preparer's Emp. Ident. or Soc. Sec. No.

☆☆☆☆ U.S. GOVERNMENT PRINTING OFFICE:1972-O-458-274   E. I. No. 23-1328538

Sample Solution

a) George must file a federal income tax return because he earned more than the $2,050 minimum income required for filing. The interest income must be added to the income from salary to find total income of $4,210.

b) See Form 1040A on page 69. The tax was found by looking down the tax table to gross income "at least $4,200 but less than $4,250, and then across to the column headed "Single, not head of household". This shows a tax of $343.

The front of Short Form 1040A is at the top, and the back of the form is shown below it.

Problems

1. Tom earned wages of $3,500 last year. He also earned $40 interest on money in his savings bank. He is single and claims one exemption. His employer deducted $228 from his pay for federal withholding tax.
   a) Does Tom owe additional tax, or is he entitled to a refund? How much?
   b) Prepare his federal income tax return on Short Form 1040A.

2. Henry earned wages of $2,850 last year. He also earned $30 interest on money in his savings bank. He is single and claims one exemption. His employer deducted $119 from his pay for federal withholding tax.
   a) Does Henry owe additional tax, or is he entitled to a refund? How much?
   b) Prepare his federal income tax return on Short Form 1040A.

3. In each of the following problems find the tax and the amount of refund or additional tax. Each person claims one exemption and is single.

	Wage Income	Interest Income	Withheld from Wages
a)	$3000	—	$ 143
b)	4300	—	365
c)	5800	$75	650
d)	7500	60	995
e)	8700	75	1270
f)	9500	80	1425
g)	8220	—	1160
h)	9130	$140	1375
i)	4200	—	338
j)	5775	$ 30	702

SECTION 3 Federal Income Tax: Income $10,000 and Over; Standard Deduction

Class Drill

1. Find 17% of $ 3,200
2. Find 19% of $ 4,300
3. Find 22% of $ 9,175
4. Find 25% of $14,400
5. Find 28% of $18,500
6. Find 32% of $21,000

7. Find 36% of $27,200   9. Find 10% of $ 1,560

8. Find 10% of $ 1,200   10. Find 10% of $ 2,475

Sample Problem

Mr. Benton earned $12,500 last year. He is married and has 2 children.

    a) Find the federal tax, if Mr. Benton does not wish to itemize his various deductions.

    b) If Mr. Benton's employer withheld $1,315 last year, should Mr. Benton ask for a refund on his tax return, or must he pay additional tax? How much?

Explanation

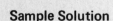

We cannot find the tax in the Tax Table because the Table is only for incomes under $10,000. This means that we must compute the tax.

We learned previously that the income tax is based on the ability to pay. We learned that the amount of tax depends on the income and the number of exemptions. The more the income, the higher the tax. If two persons have the same income, the one with fewer exemptions pays more tax.

The government also considers some other factors in determining ability to pay. If a person has high medical bills, he pays less tax. If he has high interest expenses, charity contributions, or tax expenses, he pays less income tax.

What are "high" interest expenses, medical expenses, contributions to charity or taxes? The government allows a set percentage of a person's income to be deducted for these four expenses. This deduction is known as the "*standard deduction.*" If the total of the actual expenses for interest, medical expense, contributions to charity, and taxes were more than the standard deduction, the person may list his actual expenses; if they were less, the person may show the standard deduction. The standard deduction is 15% of income, up to a maximum deduction of $2,000. If a person decides to list his deductions, he would not use the standard deduction.

For each exemption, the person may deduct $750. Thus, the more exemptions a person has, the lower his tax will be.

After deducting the standard deduction and the amount for exemptions, the remaining figure is called the "*taxable income*" because this is the figure that is used to find the tax. It is shown on line 18 on the front of Short Form 1040A.

A table of rates is used to find the amount of the tax. (See page 72.) Note that separate rates are used for single and married taxpayers. The rate for single taxpayers is shown at the left under "Schedule X" and for married taxpayers under "Schedule Y." We shall assume that all married taxpayers wish to file a "joint return", that is, one return for both husband and wife.

Sample Solution

    a) To find the taxable income, first find the standard deduction, as follows:

```
        $12500  Income
X           .15
        62500
      $12500
      1875.00  Standard Deduction
```

1972 Tax Rate Schedules

If you do not use one of the Tax Tables, figure your tax on the amount on Short Form 1040A, line 18, by using the appropriate Tax Rate Schedule on this page. Enter tax on Short Form 1040A, line 19.

SCHEDULE X—Single Taxpayers Not Qualifying for Rates in Schedule Y or Z

If the amount on Form 1040A, line 18, is: — Enter on Form 1040A, line 19:

Not over $500 ..... 14% of the amount on line 18.

Over—	But not over—		of excess over—
$500	$1,000	$70+15%	$500
$1,000	$1,500	$145+16%	$1,000
$1,500	$2,000	$225+17%	$1,500
$2,000	$4,000	$310+19%	$2,000
$4,000	$6,000	$690+21%	$4,000
$6,000	$8,000	$1,110+24%	$6,000
$8,000	$10,000	$1,590+25%	$8,000
$10,000	$12,000	$2,090+27%	$10,000
$12,000	$14,000	$2,630+29%	$12,000
$14,000	$16,000	$3,210+31%	$14,000
$16,000	$18,000	$3,830+34%	$16,000
$18,000	$20,000	$4,510+36%	$18,000
$20,000	$22,000	$5,230+38%	$20,000
$22,000	$26,000	$5,990+40%	$22,000
$26,000	$32,000	$7,590+45%	$26,000
$32,000	$38,000	$10,290+50%	$32,000
$38,000	$44,000	$13,290+55%	$38,000
$44,000	$50,000	$16,590+60%	$44,000
$50,000	$60,000	$20,190+62%	$50,000
$60,000	$70,000	$26,390+64%	$60,000
$70,000	$80,000	$32,790+66%	$70,000
$80,000	$90,000	$39,390+68%	$80,000
$90,000	$100,000	$46,190+69%	$90,000
$100,000	....	$53,090+70%	$100,000

SCHEDULE Y—Married Taxpayers and Certain Widows and Widowers

If you are a married person living apart from your wife (husband), see page 6, paragraph 1(d), of the instructions to see if you can be considered to be "unmarried" for purposes of using Schedule X or Z.

Married Taxpayers Filing Joint Returns and Certain Widows and Widowers (See page 6)

If the amount on Form 1040A, line 18, is: — Enter on Form 1040A, line 19:

Not over $1,000 ..... 14% of the amount on line 18.

Over—	But not over—		of excess over—
$1,000	$2,000	$140+15%	$1,000
$2,000	$3,000	$290+16%	$2,000
$3,000	$4,000	$450+17%	$3,000
$4,000	$8,000	$620+19%	$4,000
$8,000	$12,000	$1,380+22%	$8,000
$12,000	$16,000	$2,260+25%	$12,000
$16,000	$20,000	$3,260+28%	$16,000
$20,000	$24,000	$4,380+32%	$20,000
$24,000	$28,000	$5,660+36%	$24,000
$28,000	$32,000	$7,100+39%	$28,000
$32,000	$36,000	$8,660+42%	$32,000
$36,000	$40,000	$10,340+45%	$36,000
$40,000	$44,000	$12,140+48%	$40,000
$44,000	$52,000	$14,060+50%	$44,000
$52,000	$64,000	$18,060+53%	$52,000
$64,000	$76,000	$24,420+55%	$64,000
$76,000	$88,000	$31,020+58%	$76,000
$88,000	$100,000	$37,980+60%	$88,000
$100,000	$120,000	$45,180+62%	$100,000
$120,000	$140,000	$57,580+64%	$120,000
$140,000	$160,000	$70,380+66%	$140,000
$160,000	$180,000	$83,580+68%	$160,000
$180,000	$200,000	$97,180+69%	$180,000
$200,000	....	$110,980+70%	$200,000

Married Taxpayers Filing Separate Returns

If the amount on Form 1040A, line 18, is: — Enter on Form 1040A, line 19:

Not over $500 ..... 14% of the amount on line 18.

Over—	But not over—		of excess over—
$500	$1,000	$70+15%	$500
$1,000	$1,500	$145+16%	$1,000
$1,500	$2,000	$225+17%	$1,500
$2,000	$4,000	$310+19%	$2,000
$4,000	$6,000	$690+22%	$4,000
$6,000	$8,000	$1,130+25%	$6,000
$8,000	$10,000	$1,630+28%	$8,000
$10,000	$12,000	$2,190+32%	$10,000
$12,000	$14,000	$2,830+36%	$12,000
$14,000	$16,000	$3,550+39%	$14,000
$16,000	$18,000	$4,330+42%	$16,000
$18,000	$20,000	$5,170+45%	$18,000
$20,000	$22,000	$6,070+48%	$20,000
$22,000	$26,000	$7,030+50%	$22,000
$26,000	$32,000	$9,030+53%	$26,000
$32,000	$38,000	$12,210+55%	$32,000
$38,000	$44,000	$15,510+58%	$38,000
$44,000	$50,000	$18,990+60%	$44,000
$50,000	$60,000	$22,590+62%	$50,000
$60,000	$70,000	$28,790+64%	$60,000
$70,000	$80,000	$35,190+66%	$70,000
$80,000	$90,000	$41,790+68%	$80,000
$90,000	$100,000	$48,590+69%	$90,000
$100,000	....	$55,490+70%	$100,000

SCHEDULE Z—Unmarried (or legally separated) Taxpayers Who Qualify as Heads of Household (See page 6)

If the amount on Form 1040A, line 18, is: — Enter on Form 1040A, line 19:

Not over $1,000 ..... 14% of the amount on line 18.

Over—	But not over—		of excess over—
$1,000	$2,000	$140+16%	$1,000
$2,000	$4,000	$300+18%	$2,000
$4,000	$6,000	$660+19%	$4,000
$6,000	$8,000	$1,040+22%	$6,000
$8,000	$10,000	$1,480+23%	$8,000
$10,000	$12,000	$1,940+25%	$10,000
$12,000	$14,000	$2,440+27%	$12,000
$14,000	$16,000	$2,980+28%	$14,000
$16,000	$18,000	$3,540+31%	$16,000
$18,000	$20,000	$4,160+32%	$18,000
$20,000	$22,000	$4,800+35%	$20,000
$22,000	$24,000	$5,500+36%	$22,000
$24,000	$26,000	$6,220+38%	$24,000
$26,000	$28,000	$6,980+41%	$26,000
$28,000	$32,000	$7,800+42%	$28,000
$32,000	$36,000	$9,480+45%	$32,000
$36,000	$38,000	$11,280+48%	$36,000
$38,000	$40,000	$12,240+51%	$38,000
$40,000	$44,000	$13,260+52%	$40,000
$44,000	$50,000	$15,340+55%	$44,000
$50,000	$52,000	$18,640+56%	$50,000
$52,000	$64,000	$19,760+58%	$52,000
$64,000	$70,000	$26,720+59%	$64,000
$70,000	$76,000	$30,260+61%	$70,000
$76,000	$80,000	$33,920+62%	$76,000
$80,000	$88,000	$36,400+63%	$80,000
$88,000	$100,000	$41,440+64%	$88,000
$100,000	$120,000	$49,120+66%	$100,000
$120,000	$140,000	$62,320+67%	$120,000
$140,000	$160,000	$75,720+68%	$140,000
$160,000	$180,000	$89,320+69%	$160,000
$180,000	....	$103,120+70%	$180,000

Then deduct the standard deduction and amount for exemptions as follows:

$12500 Income
  1875 Standard Deduction
10625
  3000 4 exemptions at $750 each
$ 7625 Taxable Income

Now apply the tax rate to the taxable income. Mr. Benton is married and files a joint return, that is, one return for himself and his wife. Look at the Rate Schedule on page 72 for married taxpayers filing a joint return. Look down the left column to:

Over	But Not Over		of excess over
$4,000	$8,000	$620 + 19%	$4,000

$7625 Taxable Income $620.00 Tax on first $4,000
- 4000   688.75 Tax on excess over $4,000
  3625 Excess over $4000   1308.75 Tax on $7625
×   .19
32625
3625
688.75 Tax on excess over $4000

b) $1315.00 Withheld
                      1308.75 Income Tax
                     $ 6.25 Refund

Problems

(Assume that a married taxpayer prepares a joint return.)

1. Find the standard deduction for taxpayers having the following incomes.
   a. $11,000   c. $10,800   e. $12,000   g. $14,000
   b. $10,500   d. $11,200   f. $12,500   h. $15,000

2. Find the amount that may be deducted from income for each of the following number of exemptions:
   a. 1 exemption   c. 3 exemptions   e. 5 exemptions
   b. 2 exemptions   d. 4 exemptions   f. 6 exemptions

3. Mr. Morton earned $11,000 last year. He is married and has 1 child.
   a. Find his taxable income.
   b. Find his federal tax. (Remember to use the rate table for married persons filing a joint return.)
   c. If $1,220 was taken out of his pay last year for federal withholding tax, must he pay additional tax or will he ask for a refund? How much?

4. Mr. Randazzi earned $14,000 last year. He is married and has 3 children.
   a. Find his taxable income. (Reminder: standard deduction has maximum of $2000)
   b. Find his federal tax.
   c. If $1,500 was taken out of his pay for federal withholding tax, will he ask for a refund or must he pay additional tax? How much?

5. After subtracting his standard deduction and exemption allowance, Julio had a taxable income last year of $9,000. If he is single, find his federal income tax. (Remember to use the rate schedule for a single person.)

6. After subtracting his standard deduction and exemption allowance, Tony had a taxable income of $9,400. If he is single, find his federal income tax.

7. After subtracting his standard deduction and exemption allowance, Sam had a taxable income last year of $10,200. If he is single, find his federal income tax.

8. Sam's friend, Bill, works in the same firm, and had the same taxable income as Sam: $10,200. (See Example 7)
   a. If Bill is married, find his federal income tax.
   b. Why is the tax different from Sam's tax?

9. Mr. Reilly's salary last year was $12,200. He had interest from savings of $100. He is married and has 5 children.
   a. Find his taxable income.
   b. Find his federal income tax.

10. Mr. Rodriguez earned a salary last year of $17,400. He had interest from savings of $150. He is married and has 4 children.
    a) Find his taxable income.
    b) Find his federal income tax.

11. Mr. Townley has two sons. Bill is 17 years old and Jim is 18. Bill earned $700 last year, and Jim earned $900. Both live at home and are supported by Mr. Townley. May he claim them as exemptions when he files his tax return? Why?

SECTION 4   Federal Income Tax: Listing Deductions; Form 1040

Class Drill

1. Find 19% of $2,400
2. Find 22% of $1,300
3. Find 28% of $1,500
4. Find 10% of $1,250

5. Find 10% of $1,470
6. Find 10% of $2,150

7. Find 5% of $3,200
8. Find 1% of $1,250

Sample Problem

Mr. Harris earned $6,500 last year. He is single, with one exemption. He gave $400 to charity, paid $900 for real estate taxes on his home, and $800 for interest on his mortgage.

a. Should he use the tax table for incomes under $10,000? Give reason.
b. Find his income tax.

Explanation

When the Internal Revenue Service prepared the tax tables, it took into consideration the standard deduction allowed to taxpayers. It allowed 15% of gross income for contributions, taxes, medical expense and interest expense up to a maximum of $2,000.

If actual expenses were greater than the standard deduction allowed in the table, then the taxpayer should list his actual expenses in order to lower his tax.

In order to help taxpayers with low incomes, the government established, in 1970, a new "low-income allowance", which may be used instead of the standard deduction explained above. The low income allowance is $1,300.

The Internal Revenue Service considered both the standard deduction and the low income allowance when it prepared the Tax Tables. It used whichever method would be of greater help to the taxpayer.

To sum up: If actual expenses were greater than the standard deduction or the low income allowance, then the taxpayer should list his deductions. This would usually be true if the taxpayer had large medical expenses, or owned his own home and had large interest and tax expenses. It is best to list the deductions in these cases:

If Income is	List Deduction when
Up to $8,666	Over $1,300
From $8,667 to $13,333	Over 15% of income
Over $13,333	Over $2,000

If deductions are itemized on the tax return, Short Form 1040A cannot be used. The long form, called Form 1040, must be used. The deductions are shown on a separate page of the tax return, called "Schedule A - Itemized Deductions." (see pages 77–79.)

Sample Solution

a. Mr. Harris should not use the Tax Table because he had large deductions amounting to more than the standard deduction or the low income allowance. His deductions total more than $1,300.
b. Mr. Harris would prepare Schedule A (see page 79). He would complete his Form 1040 as follows:

Income	$6,500
Deductions	2,100
	4,400
1 exemption	750
Taxable Income	$3,650

75

Over	But Not Over		of excess over
$2,000	$4,000	$310 + 19%	$2,000

$3650	Taxable Income	$310.00 Tax on first $2,000
− 2000		313.50 Tax on excess over $2,000
1650	Excess over $2,000	$623.50 Tax
× .19		
14850		
1650		
313.50	Tax on excess	

If Mr. Harris had used the Tax Table (see page 68), his tax would have been $790.00. By listing his deductions, therefore, he saved the difference between $790.00 and his actual tax of $623.50, or $166.50.

Problems Group A

Group A — Income less than $10,000

In each of the following problems, the person is single with one exemption.
a. Should he list his deductions on Form 1040, or use the Tax Table and Short Form 1040A? Why?
b. If he should list his deductions, find his taxable income, and then use the rates to find the tax.
c. If he should use the Tax Table, find his tax from the Table.

	INCOME		DEDUCTIONS		
		Interest Expense	Real Estate Tax	Contributions	Allowable Medical Expense
1.	$8,000	$1,300	$500	$200	—
2.	9,000	800	600	500	—
3.	6,500	750	400	100	$ 800
4.	5,400	—	—	300	$1,200
5.	2,100	—	—	100	200
6.	2,300	—	—	200	300

Problems Group B

Group B — Income $10,000 and over

7. Mr. Thompson earned $12,000 last year. He is single. Last year he spent $800 for contributions to various organized charities, and $1,100 for interest expense.
a. Should he list his deductions or take the standard deduction?
b. Find his taxable income.
c. Find his tax.

8. Mr. Davis earned $14,500 last year. He is married and has 1 child. He paid $900 in real estate taxes on his home, and $1,200 in interest on his home mortgage.
a. Should he list his deductions or take the standard deduction?
b. Find his taxable income.
c. Find his tax.

Form **1040**

US Department of the Treasury / Internal Revenue Service
Individual Income Tax Return 1972

For the year January 1–December 31, 1972, or other taxable year beginning ...., 1972, ending ...., 19......

Please print or type	First name and initial (If joint return, use first names and middle initials of both) SAMUEL G Last name HARRIS Your social security number (Husband's, if joint return) 291 73 0435

Present home address (Number and street, including apartment number, or rural route)
1415 BROADWAY   Wife's number, if joint return

City, town or post office, State and ZIP code
LONG ISLAND CITY, N.Y. 11103   Occupation   Yours CLERK   Wife's

Filing Status—check only one:

1 ☑ Single
2 ☐ Married filing joint return (even if only one had income)
3 ☐ Married filing separately. If wife (husband) is also filing give her (his) social security number and first name here.

4 ☐ Unmarried Head of Household
5 ☐ Widow(er) with dependent child (Enter year of death of husband (wife) ▶ 19   )

Exemptions   Regular / 65 or over / Blind   Enter number of boxes checked

6 Yourself . . . . . ☑ ☐ ☐ ▶ 1
7 Wife (husband) . . . ☐ ☐ ☐
8 First names of your dependent children who lived with you _____

9 Number of other dependents (from line 32) . . . ▶
10 Total exemptions claimed . . . . ▶   1

Income

11	Wages, salaries, tips, and other employee compensation. (Attach Form W–2 to front. If unavailable, attach explanation) ·	11	6500 00
12a	Dividends (see pages 6 and 13 of instr.) $ .... 12b Less exclusion $ .... Balance ▶	12c	
	(If gross dividends and other distributions are over $200, list in Part I of Schedule B.)		
13	Interest income. [If $200 or less, enter total without listing in Schedule B] [If over $200, enter total and list in Part II of Schedule B] ·	13	
14	Income other than wages, dividends, and interest (from line 45)	14	
15	Total (add lines 11, 12c, 13 and 14)	15	6500 00
16	Adjustments to income (such as "sick pay," moving expenses, etc. from line 50) .	16	
17	Subtract line 16 from line 15 (adjusted gross income)	17	6500 00

● **Caution:** If you have unearned income and you could be claimed as a dependent on your parent's return, see boxed instruction on page 7, under the heading "Tax-Credits-Payments." Check this block ☐.

● If you do not itemize deductions and line 17 is under $10,000, find tax in Tables and enter on line 18.

● If you itemize deductions or line 17 is $10,000 or more, go to line 51 to figure tax.

Tax, Payments and Credits

18	Tax, check if from: — Tax Tables 1–12, Schedule D ✓ Tax Rate Schedule X, Y, or Z Schedule G or Form 4726	18	623 50
19	Total credits (from line 61)	19	
20	Income tax (subtract line 19 from line 18)	20	623 50
21	Other taxes (from line 67)	21	
22	Total (add lines 20 and 21)	22	623 50
23	Total Federal income tax withheld (attach Forms W–2 or W–2P to front) 23 625 00		
24	1972 Estimated tax payments (include amount allowed as credit from 1971 return) 24		
25	Amount paid with Form 4868, Application for Automatic Extension of Time to File U.S. Individual Income Tax Return 25		
26	Other payments (from line 71) 26		
27	Total (add lines 23, 24, 25, and 26)	27	625 00

Bal. Due or Refund

28	If line 22 is larger than line 27, enter BALANCE DUE IRS Pay in full with return. Make check or money order payable to Internal Revenue Service ▶	28	
29	If line 27 is larger than line 22, enter amount OVERPAID . . . . ▶	29	1 50
30	Line 29 to be REFUNDED TO YOU . . . . ▶	30	1 50
31	Line 29 to be credited on 1973 estimated tax 31		

Foreign Accounts

Did you, at any time during the taxable year, have any interest in or signature or other authority over a bank, securities, or other financial account in a foreign country (except in a U.S. military banking facility operated by a U.S. financial institution)? . . . . ▶ ☐ Yes ☑ No
If "Yes," attach Form 4683. (For definitions, see Form 4683.)

Note: Be sure to complete Revenue Sharing (lines 33 and 34) on next page.

Under penalties of perjury, I declare that I have examined this return, including accompanying schedules and statements, and to the best of my knowledge and belief it is true, correct, and complete. Declaration of preparer (other than taxpayer) is based on all information of which he has any knowledge.

Sign here ▶ _Samuel G Harris_   3/1/73   Date   ▶ Preparer's signature (other than taxpayer)   Date

Your signature   Wife's (husband's) signature (if filing jointly, BOTH must sign even if only one had income)   Address (and ZIP Code)   Preparer's Emp. Ident. or Soc. Sec. No.

Front of Form 1040

Form 1040 (1972)   Page **2**

<table>
<tr><td rowspan="2">**Other Dependents**</td><td>(a) NAME</td><td>(b) Relationship</td><td>(c) Months lived in your home. If born or died during year, write B or D.</td><td>(d) Did dependent have income of $750 or more?</td><td>(e) Amount YOU furnished for dependent's support. If 100% write ALL.</td><td>(f) Amount furnished by OTHERS including dependent.</td></tr>
<tr><td></td><td></td><td></td><td></td><td>$</td><td>$</td></tr>
</table>

32 Total number of dependents listed in column (a). Enter here and on line 9 . . . . ▶

Revenue Sharing

33 Print or type the location of your principal place of residence at end of year (not necessarily the same as your post office address).

(a) State	(b) County	(c) Locality. If you lived inside the boundaries of an incorporated city, town, etc., enter its name; if not, check here ▶ ☐	(d) Township (see instructions on page 8)
N Y	QUEENS	NEW YORK CITY	

34 Enter the number of persons included on line 10 who (1) are filing a return of their own; or, (2) did not live at your principal place of residence at the end of the year . . . . ▶   //// For IRS use only—Leave blank ////

PART I.—Income other than Wages, Dividends, and Interest

35 Business income (or loss) (attach Schedule C)	35	
36 Net gain (or loss) from sale or exchange of capital assets (attach Schedule D)	36	
37 Net gain (or loss) from Supplemental Schedule of Gains and Losses (attach Form 4797) . . .	37	
38 Pensions and annuities, rents and royalties, partnerships, estates or trusts, etc. (attach Schedule E)	38	
39 Farm income (or loss) (attach Schedule F)	39	
40 Fully taxable pensions and annuities (not reported on Schedule E—see instructions on page 8) .	40	
41 50% of capital gain distributions (not reported on Schedule D)	41	
42 State income tax refunds (caution—see instructions on page 8)	42	
43 Alimony	43	
44 Other (state nature and source)	44	
45 Total (add lines 35 through 44). Enter here and on line 14 . . . . ▶	45	

PART II.—Adjustments to Income

46 "Sick pay" if included in income (attach Form 2440 or other required statement)	46	
47 Moving expense (attach Form 3903)	47	
48 Employee business expense (attach Form 2106 or other statement)	48	
49 Payments as a self-employed person to a retirement plan, etc. (see Form 4848)	49	
50 Total adjustments (add lines 46, 47, 48, and 49). Enter here and on line 16 . . . . . ▶	50	

PART III.—Tax Computation (Do not use this part if you use Tax Tables 1–12 to find your tax.)

51 Adjusted gross income (from line 17)	51	6500	00
52 (a) If you itemize deductions, enter total from Schedule A, line 40 and attach Schedule A	52	2100	00
(b) If you do not itemize deductions, enter 15% of line 51, but do NOT enter more than $2,000. ($1,000 if line 3 is checked)			
53 Subtract line 52 from line 51	53	4400	00
54 Multiply total number of exemptions claimed on line 10, by $750	54	750	00
55 Taxable income. Subtract line 54 from line 53	55	3650	00

(Figure your tax on the amount on line 55 by using Tax Rate Schedule X, Y or Z, or if applicable, the alternative tax from Schedule D, income averaging from Schedule G, or maximum tax from Form 4726.) Enter tax on line 18.

PART IV.—Credits

56 Retirement income credit (attach Schedule R)	56	
57 Investment credit (attach Form 3468)	57	
58 Foreign tax credit (attach Form 1116)	58	
59 Credit for contributions to candidates for public office—see instructions on page 9 . . .	59	
60 Work Incentive Program credit (attach Form 4874)	60	
61 Total credits (add lines 56, 57, 58, 59, and 60). Enter here and on line 19 . . . . . ▶	61	

PART V.—Other Taxes

62 Self-employment tax (attach Schedule SE)	62	
63 Tax from recomputing prior-year investment credit (attach Form 4255)	63	
64 Minimum tax (see instructions on page 10). Check here ☐, if Form 4625 is attached . . .	64	
65 Social security tax on tip income not reported to employer (attach Form 4137)	65	
66 Uncollected employee social security tax on tips (from Forms W–2)	66	
67 Total (add lines 62, 63, 64, 65, and 66). Enter here and on line 21 . . . . . . ▶	67	

PART VI.—Other Payments

68 Excess FICA tax withheld (two or more employers—see instructions on page 10)	68	
69 Credit for Federal tax on special fuels, nonhighway gasoline and lubricating oil (attach Form 4136)	69	
70 Credit from a Regulated Investment Company (attach Form 2439)	70	
71 Total (add lines 68, 69, and 70). Enter here and on line 26 . . . . ▶	71	

☆☆☆☆U.S. GOVERNMENT PRINTING OFFICE: 1972-O-459-271   (82615-388)

Back of Form 1040

78

Schedules A&B—Itemized Deductions AND Dividend and Interest Income

(Form 1040)
Department of the Treasury
Internal Revenue Service ▶ Attach to Form 1040.

1972

Name(s) as shown on Form 1040

SAM HARRIS

Your social security number
291 73 0435

Schedule A—Itemized Deductions (Schedule B on back)

Medical and dental expenses (not compensated by insurance or otherwise) for medicine and drugs, doctors, dentists, nurses, hospital care, insurance premiums for medical care, etc.

1 One half (but not more than $150) of insurance premiums for medical care. (Be sure to include in line 10 below) . . .

2 Medicine and drugs . . . . . .

3 Enter 1% of line 17, Form 1040 . . .

4 Subtract line 3 from line 2. Enter difference (if less than zero, enter zero) . .

5 Enter balance of insurance premiums for medical care not entered on line 1 . .

6 Itemize other medical and dental expenses. Include hearing aids, dentures, eyeglasses, transportation, etc.

7 Total (add lines 4, 5, and 6) . . . .

8 Enter 3% of line 17, Form 1040 . . .

9 Subtract line 8 from line 7. Enter difference (if less than zero, enter zero) . .

10 Total deductible medical and dental expenses (Add lines 1 and 9. Enter here and on line 33, below.) . . . . . ▶

Taxes.

11 Real estate . . . . | 900 00

12 State and local gasoline (see gas tax tables)

13 General sales (see sales tax tables) . .

14 State and local income . . . . . .

15 Personal property . . . .

16 Other

17 Total taxes (Add lines 11 through 16. Enter here and on line 34, below.). ▶ | 900 00

Contributions.—Cash—including checks, money orders, etc. (Itemize—see instructions on page 11 for examples.)

RED CROSS | 400 00

18 Total cash contributions . . . . . | 400 00

19 Other than cash (see instructions on page 12 for required statement). Enter total for such items here . . . .

20 Carryover from prior years . . . .

21 Total contributions (Add lines 18, 19, and 20. Enter here and on line 35, below.) ▶ | 400 00

Interest expense.

22 Home mortgage . . . . | 800 00

23 Installment purchases . . . . . .

24 Other (Itemize)

25 Total interest expense (Add lines 22, 23 and 24. Enter here and on line 36, below.) . . . . ▶ | 800 00

Casualty or theft loss(es)
See instructions on page 12. NOTE: If you had more than one casualty or theft loss occurrence, OMIT lines 26 through 29 and see page 12 of the instructions for guidance.

26 Loss before adjustments . . . . .

27 Insurance reimbursement . . . .

28 $100 limitation . . . . | $100 00

29 Add lines 27 and 28 . . . .

30 Casualty or theft loss. (Excess of line 26 over line 29. Enter here and on line 37, below.) . . . . ▶

31 Child and dependent care expenses from Form 2441. (Enter here and on line 38, below.) . . . . . . ▶

Miscellaneous deductions for alimony, union dues, etc. (see instructions on page 13).

32 Total miscellaneous deductions (Enter here and on line 39, below.) . . . ▶

Summary of Itemized Deductions A

33 Total deductible medical and dental expenses (from line 10) . . . .

34 Total taxes (from line 17) . . . . | 900 00

35 Total contributions (from line 21) . . . . | 400 00

36 Total interest expense (from line 25) . . . . | 800 00

37 Casualty and theft loss(es) (from line 30) . . . .

38 Child and dependent care expenses (from line 31) . . . .

39 Total miscellaneous deductions (from line 32) . . . .

40 TOTAL ITEMIZED DEDUCTIONS. (Add lines 33 through 39. Enter here and on Form 1040, line 52.) . . ▶ | 2100 00

Schedule A, Form 1040

9. Mr. Keily earned $15,200 last year. He is married, and has two children. He paid $600 in real estate taxes and $500 in interest on his mortgage.
   a. Should he list his deductions or take the standard deduction?
   b. Find his taxable income.
   c. Find his tax.

10. Mr. Abrams is single. He earned $11,800 last year. He paid $400 for allowable medical expense, and gave $540 to various organized charities.
    a. Should he list his deductions or take the standard deduction?
    b. Find his taxable income.
    c. Find his federal tax.

11. Mr. Johnson is married, and has 1 child. He earned $17,000 last year. He paid $750 in real estate taxes, $920 in interest, and gave $530 to charity.
    a. Should he list his deductions or take the standard deduction?
    b. Find his taxable income.
    c. Find his federal income tax.

SECTION 5   New York State Income Tax: Short Form

Class Drill

1. Find 10% of $147
2. Find 1% of $243
3. Find 150% of $600
4. Find 1/2% of $50

5. Multiply $85 by 10
6. Multiply $86.43 by 10
7. Divide $65 by 10
8. Divide $175.80 by 10

Sample Problem

Mr. Davis earned $6,500 last year. He is single.
a) Find his New York State Income Tax.
b) Prepare his New York State tax return, if $161 was withheld from his pay for the New York State income tax.

Explanation

The New York State tax law requires that a New York State tax return must be filed by every individual required to file a Federal income tax return, or if total New York income exceeds the number of exemptions multiplied by $650.

There are two kinds of returns, similar to the federal returns. The short form is known as IT200, and may be used when total income is less than $15,000, and consists of wages, and no more than $1,000 of interest and dividends, and the standard deduction is used.

The tax is found from the Tax Table. A portion of the 1972 table for single persons is shown on the next page.

80

(Head of Household, Surviving Spouse with dependent child and Married persons filing a joint return use Table B. Married persons filing separate returns must use Form IT-201 or IT-208.)

HOW TO USE TABLE A

Read down the TOTAL NY INCOME columns below and find the line covering the TOTAL NEW YORK INCOME reported on Line 6 of Form IT-200. Read across to the column headed by the number of exemptions claimed on Line 1 of Form IT-200. The tax stated here is the amount to be entered on Line 8 of Form IT-200. Single persons with total New York income of $2,500 or less owe no tax. Enter zero on Line 8. Be sure to check the "single" box on Line 7.

This Tax Table reflects an exemption of $650 per year for each exemption claimed. The 14% Standard Deduction up to $2,000 or the Minimum Standard Deduction of $1,000, whichever is greater, is allowed. The tax shown to be due on this Tax Table includes the tax surcharge of 2½%. The exemption from tax for a single individual having New York adjusted gross income of $2,500 or less is also reflected in this Tax Table.

IF TOTAL NY INCOME ON LINE 6 IS:		AND THE NUMBER OF EXEMPTIONS CLAIMED IS:									10 OR OVER NO TAX
At Least	But Less Than	1	2	3	4	5	6	7	8	9	
$3600	$3650	$50	$30	$14	$1	$0	$0	$0	$0	$0	$0
3650	3700	52	32	15	2	0	0	0	0	0	0
3700	3750	54	34	16	3	0	0	0	0	0	0
3750	3800	55	35	17	4	0	0	0	0	0	0
3800	3850	57	37	18	5	0	0	0	0	0	0
3850	3900	58	38	19	6	0	0	0	0	0	0
3900	3950	60	40	20	7	0	0	0	0	0	0
3950	4000	61	41	21	8	0	0	0	0	0	0
4000	4050	63	43	23	9	0	0	0	0	0	0
4050	4100	64	44	24	10	0	0	0	0	0	0
4100	4150	66	46	26	11	0	0	0	0	0	0
4150	4200	67	47	27	12	0	0	0	0	0	0
4200	4250	69	49	29	13	0	0	0	0	0	0
4250	4300	70	50	30	14	1	0	0	0	0	0
4300	4350	72	52	32	15	2	0	0	0	0	0
4350	4400	74	54	34	16	3	0	0	0	0	0
4400	4450	75	55	35	17	4	0	0	0	0	0
4450	4500	77	57	37	18	5	0	0	0	0	0
4500	4550	78	58	38	19	6	0	0	0	0	0
4550	4600	80	60	40	20	7	0	0	0	0	0
4600	4650	81	61	41	21	8	0	0	0	0	0
4650	4700	83	63	43	23	9	0	0	0	0	0
4700	4750	85	64	44	24	10	0	0	0	0	0
4750	4800	87	66	46	26	11	0	0	0	0	0
4800	4850	89	67	47	27	12	0	0	0	0	0
4850	4900	91	69	49	29	13	0	0	0	0	0
4900	4950	93	70	50	30	14	1	0	0	0	0
4950	5000	95	72	52	32	15	2	0	0	0	0
5000	5050	97	74	54	34	16	3	0	0	0	0
5050	5100	99	75	55	35	17	4	0	0	0	0
5100	5150	101	77	57	37	18	5	0	0	0	0
5150	5200	104	78	58	38	19	6	0	0	0	0
5200	5250	106	80	60	40	20	7	0	0	0	0
5250	5300	108	81	61	41	21	8	0	0	0	0
5300	5350	110	83	63	43	23	9	0	0	0	0
5350	5400	112	85	64	44	24	10	0	0	0	0
5400	5450	114	87	66	46	26	11	0	0	0	0
5450	5500	116	89	67	47	27	12	0	0	0	0
5500	5550	118	91	69	49	29	13	0	0	0	0
5550	5600	120	93	70	50	30	14	1	0	0	0
5600	5650	122	95	72	52	32	15	2	0	0	0
5650	5700	124	97	74	54	34	16	3	0	0	0
5700	5750	126	99	75	55	35	17	4	0	0	0
5750	5800	128	101	77	57	37	18	5	0	0	0
5800	5850	130	104	78	58	38	19	6	0	0	0
5850	5900	132	106	80	60	40	20	7	0	0	0
5900	5950	134	108	81	61	41	21	8	0	0	0
5950	6000	136	110	83	63	43	23	9	0	0	0
6000	6050	138	112	85	64	44	24	10	0	0	0
6050	6100	140	114	87	66	46	26	11	0	0	0
6100	6150	142	116	89	67	47	27	12	0	0	0
6150	6200	145	118	91	69	49	29	13	0	0	0
6200	6250	147	120	93	70	50	30	14	1	0	0
6250	6300	149	122	95	72	52	32	15	2	0	0
6300	6350	151	124	97	74	54	34	16	3	0	0
6350	6400	153	126	99	75	55	35	17	4	0	0
6400	6450	155	128	101	77	57	37	18	5	0	0
6450	6500	157	130	104	78	58	38	19	6	0	0
6500	6550	159	132	106	80	60	40	20	7	0	0
6550	6600	161	134	108	81	61	41	21	8	0	0
6600	6650	163	136	110	83	63	43	23	9	0	0
6650	6700	165	138	112	85	64	44	24	10	0	0
6700	6750	168	140	114	87	66	46	26	11	0	0
6750	6800	170	142	116	89	67	47	27	12	0	0
6800	6850	173	145	118	91	69	49	29	13	0	0
6850	6900	176	147	120	93	70	50	30	14	1	0
6900	6950	178	149	122	95	72	52	32	15	2	0
6950	7000	181	151	124	97	74	54	34	16	3	0
7000	7050	183	153	126	99	75	55	35	17	4	0
7050	7100	186	155	128	101	77	57	37	18	5	0
7100	7150	188	157	130	104	78	58	38	19	6	0
7150	7200	191	159	132	105	80	60	40	20	7	0
7200	7250	193	160	134	107	81	61	41	21	7	0
7250	7300	195	162	136	109	82	62	42	22	8	0
7300	7350	197	164	137	111	84	64	44	24	9	0
7350	7400	199	166	139	112	86	65	45	25	10	0
7400	7450	202	168	141	114	88	66	46	26	11	0
7450	7500	204	171	143	116	89	68	48	28	12	0
7500	7550	206	173	144	118	91	69	49	29	13	0
7550	7600	208	175	146	119	93	70	50	30	14	0

IF TOTAL NY INCOME ON LINE 6 IS:		AND THE NUMBER OF EXEMPTIONS CLAIMED IS:			4 OR OVER NO TAX
At Least	But Less Than	1	2	3	
$ 0	$2500.01	$0	$0	$0	$0
2500.01	2525	18	4	0	0
2525	2550	18	5	0	0
2550	2575	19	5	0	0
2575	2600	19	6	0	0
2600	2625	20	6	0	0
2625	2650	20	7	0	0
2650	2675	21	7	0	0
2675	2700	22	8	0	0
2700	2725	22	8	0	0
2725	2750	23	9	0	0
2750	2775	24	9	0	0
2775	2800	25	10	0	0
2800	2825	25	11	0	0
2825	2850	26	11	0	0
2850	2875	27	12	0	0
2875	2900	28	12	0	0
2900	2925	29	13	0	0
2925	2950	29	13	0	0
2950	2975	30	14	0	0
2975	3000	31	14	1	0
3000	3050	32	15	2	0
3050	3100	34	16	3	0
3100	3150	35	17	4	0
3150	3200	37	18	5	0
3200	3250	38	19	6	0
3250	3300	40	20	7	0
3300	3350	41	21	8	0
3350	3400	43	23	9	0
3400	3450	44	24	10	0
3450	3500	46	26	11	0
3500	3550	47	27	12	0
3550	3600	49	29	13	0

Note that in the 1972 tax return, a single person with a gross income of $2,500 or less, or a married couple filing a joint return with a gross income of $5,000 or less, will pay no state income tax.

Also note that starting with the 1972 tax return, there is a 2.5% surcharge on the state income tax. This amount has been included in the table.

Sample Solution

a) His New York State income tax for 1972 is $159.00, shown in the table, on the line "at least $6,500 but less than $6,550".

b) His New York State income tax return is shown below:

IT-200	New York State Income Tax Resident Return 1972		

R To have Income Tax Bureau compute Tax enter information on lines 1, 2, 3, 4, 5, 6, 7 and 9. Sign Return below.

For reporting income less than $15,000

Married persons filing separate returns cannot use this form.
Name—If Joint Return, use first names and initials of both

GARY DAVIS

Home address—Number and street or rural route   Apt. No.

2515 32 AVE.

City, village or post office and state   ZIP code

LONG ISLAND CITY, N.Y. 11103

Your social security number   Spouse's social security number

206 | 14 | 5215

Taxpayer's county of residence

QUEENS

Sign Here ▶ *Gary Davis*   Date 3/15/73
If Joint Return, both husband and wife must sign

Signature of preparer other than taxpayer   Date

Address of preparer

1 Number of exemptions from Federal return **1**

2 Salary or wages   **6500 | 00**

3 Interest and dividends

4 Total Income (line 2 plus line 3)   **6500 | 00**

5 Subtraction for nonpublic school students (see instructions for line 5)

6 Total New York Income (line 4 less line 5)   **6500 | 00**

7 Filing Status — check only one:
☑ Single — use Table A to compute tax.
☐ Married (filing joint return) — use Table B to compute tax.
☐ Head of household or surviving spouse — use Table B to compute tax.

8 Tax on amount on line 6 (from New York State tax table)   **159 | 00**

9 Total NY State tax withheld — attach Forms IT-2102   **161 | 00**

10 If line 8 is larger than 9, enter Balance Due ▶▶▶

11 If line 9 is larger than 8, enter Refund claimed ▶▶▶   **2 | 00**

Problems

1. Joe, a student, earned $520 last year.
   a) If $4.00 was taken out of his pay for the New York State withholding tax, why should Joe file a tax return?
   b) How much refund should he request?

2. Tom earned $1900 last year. He is single.
   a) Find his New York State income tax.
   b) If his New York State withholding tax for the year was $34, will he ask for a refund, or must he pay additional tax? How much?

3. Bill earned $3,200 last year. He is single.
   a) Find his New York State income tax.
   b) If his New York State withholding tax for the year was $30, will he ask for a refund, or must he pay additional tax? How much?

4. Mr. Taylor earned $7,100 last year. He is single.
   a) Find his New York State income tax.
   b) If his New York State withholding tax amounted to $194, must he pay any additional tax, or will he ask for a refund? How much?

5. Mr. Davis earned a salary of $7,000 last year. His savings account also gave him interest of $230. He is single.
   a) Find his New York State income tax.
   b) If his New York State withholding tax for the year was $185, must he pay additional tax or will he get a refund? How much?

6. Mr. Benny earned a salary of $5,300 last year. He also earned $400 interest on his savings account. He is single.
   a) Find his New York State income tax.
   b) If his New York State withholding tax for the year was $121, must he pay additional tax or will he get a refund? How much?

SECTION 6   New York City Income Tax

Class Drill

1. Find .7% (.007) of $300	6. Find 1.1% of $2,000
2. Find .7% of $500	7. Find 1.4% of $2,500
3. Find .7% of $750	8. Find 1.4% of $3,000
4. Find .7% of $1,000	9. Find 1.8% of $2,300
5. Find 1.1% of $800	10. Find 1.8% of $4,000

Sample Problem

Mr. Davis is a resident of New York City and is subject to the New York City income tax. His salary totaled $7,000 last year. Must he file a New York City income tax form?

Explanation

A resident of New York City does not have to file a New York City tax return if he meets all of the following conditions:

1. The gross income on his Federal income tax return was not more than $8,000.

2. Not more than $300 of the income was from sources other than wages, such as interest.

3. The employer took out of his pay the correct amount of withholding tax.

If the resident does have to file a tax return, there are two kinds of returns: short form and long form. The short form may be used for income under $10,000. The amount of tax is found from a tax table in the same way that the federal and state tax was found. There is no tax on a single person who earned less than $750. If the person wishes to obtain a refund on his New York City withholding tax, he should file a tax return.

Sample Solution

Mr. Davis does not have to file a New York City tax return because he earned less than $8,000, he had no other income, and his employer took withholding tax out of his pay.

Problems

Which of the following single people should file a New York City tax return? Why?

	Income	Tax Withheld		Income	Tax Withheld
1.	$ 500	$2.00	5.	$8500	$85.00
2.	700	4.00	6.	9000	92.00
3.	5000	40.00	7.	9400	97.00
4.	7500	65.00	8.	9800	102.00

SECTION 7   Review Problems

1. Sam earned $1,400 in wages last year. He had no other income. He filed Form W-4E with his employer.
   a. *Must* he file a federal tax return? Explain.
   b. *Should* he file a federal tax return? Explain.

2. George earned $650 last year. He filed a Form W-4 with his employer. During the year $80 was deducted from his pay for federal withholding tax.
   a. *Must* George file a federal income tax return? Explain.
   b. *Should* George file a federal income tax return? Why?

3. Mr. Dale earned wages of $5,300 last year. His employer deducted $525 from his pay for federal withholding tax. Mr. Dale is single and claims one exemption.
   a. Use the tax table to find his federal income tax.
   b. Does Mr. Dale owe additional tax, or should he claim a refund? How much?

4. Mr. McGregor earned wages of $7,500 last year. He also earned $125 interest on money in his savings bank. He is single and claims one exemption. His employer deducted $1,140 from his pay for federal withholding tax.
   a. Use the tax table to find his federal income tax.
   b. Does Mr. McGregor owe additional tax, or should he claim a refund? How much?

5. Mr. Jefferson earned $12,000 last year. He is single, and claims one exemption. When preparing his federal income tax, he decided to take the standard deduction.
   a. Find his taxable income.
   b. Find his federal income tax.
   c. If $1,900 was taken out of his pay last year for federal withholding tax, must he pay additional tax or will he ask for a refund? How much?

6. Mr. Maxwell earned $14,500 last year. He is married and has one child. In addition to his $14,500 salary, he had interest on savings accounts of $400. He decided to take the standard deduction.
   a. Find his taxable income.
   b. Find his federal income tax.
   c. If $1,925 was taken out of his pay last year for the federal withholding tax, must he pay additional tax or will he obtain a refund? How much?

7. Mr. Abrams earned $7,700 last year. He is single, and claims one exemption. He gave $900 to various organized charities, and had allowable medical expenses during the year of $800.
   a. Should he use the tax table for income under $10,000 to find his tax, or should he list his deductions and use the rate table? Why?
   b. Find his taxable income, listing his deductions.
   c. Use the taxable income to find his federal income tax.
   d. If he used the tax table for income under $10,000, find his federal tax.
   e. Which method was better? How much better?

8. Mr. Greenwald earned $9,100 last year. He is single, and claims one exemption. He gave $300 to various organized charities, and had allowable medical expenses of $500.
   a. Should he use the tax table for income under $10,000 to find his federal tax, or should he list his deductions and use the rate table? Why?
   b. Find his taxable income, listing his deductions.
   c. Use the taxable income to find his federal income tax.
   d. Use the tax table for income under $10,000 to find his tax.
   e. Which method was better? How much better?

9. Mr. Rizzutto earned $14,000 last year. He is married, and has two children. He paid $800 for real estate taxes on his home, and $1,400 for interest on the mortgage on his home.
   a. Should he take the standard deduction or list his deductions? Why?
   b. Find his taxable income.
   c. Find his federal income tax.

10. Mr. Barry earned $7,300 last year. He is single and claims one exemption. He does not wish to list his deductions. Find his New York State income tax.

11. Mr. Gordon earned $7,500 last year. He is single and claims one exemption. He wishes to take the standard deduction.
    a. Which New York State income tax return should he use? Why?
    b. Find his New York State income tax.

UNIT 6
Insurance

SECTION 1 — Fire Insurance: Finding the Premium

Class Drill

1. Divide $4,300 by 100
2. Divide $5,650 by 100
3. Divide $15,475 by 100
4. Multiply: 130×2.7
5. Multiply: 55×3.25

Multiply: (answer to nearest cent)

6. $36.25	7. $52.75	8. $73.25
$\times\ .60$	$\times\ .56$	$\times\ .40$

Sample Problem

Mr. Thomas bought a $25,000 fire insurance policy on his home.
a) If the annual rate is $.15 per $100, what is the premium for a year?
b) What would Mr. Thomas have to pay for a 3 year policy?

Explanation

The cost of carrying a fire insurance policy is called the premium. This premium is found by using a rate ($.15 in above problem) for each $100 worth of insurance that is purchased. The rate varies, depending on such factors as the following:

1. How is the building constructed? (The rate for a brick building would be less than for a frame dwelling.)

2. How is the building used? (A paint factory would have a higher rate than an office building.)

3. What is near the building? (A dynamite plant next to it would increase the risk.)

4. What protection is available? (A sprinkler system would reduce the rate.)

87

In order to encourage the buyer of a fire insurance policy to buy insurance for more than one year at a time, the insurance company offers reduced rates, as follows:

Rates for More Than One Year	
Time	Rate
2 years	1.85 times the annual premium
3 years	2.70 times the annual premium
4 years	3.55 times the annual premium
5 years	4.40 times the annual premium

Sample Solution

a) To find the number of hundreds, divide $25,000 by 100. To do this, move the decimal point 2 places to the left. Then multiply by the rate for each $100 to find the premium for one year.

$250
× .15
1250
250
$37.50 Premium for 1 year.

b) Look at the table of rates for more than one year. The premium for 3 years is 2.7 times the annual premium.

$37.50
× 2.7
26250
7500
$101.250 = $101.25 Premium for 3 years

Problems

1. Find the cost of a $5,000 fire insurance policy for 1 year if the rate is $.23 per $100.

2. Find the cost of a $7,500 fire insurance policy for a year if the rate is $.34 per $100.

3. Find the annual premium in each of the following:

	Amount of Policy	Rate per $100
a.	$ 8,600	$.19
b.	$12,700	$.23
c.	$15,800	$.37
d.	$27,000	$.29
e.	$35,600	$.31
f.	$26,500	$.27

4. Mr. Smith insured his home for $27,000 at an annual rate of $.24 per $100.
   a. What is the annual premium?
   b. If Mr. Smith bought a 3 year policy, what would it cost him?

5. Mr. Turner bought a $35,000 fire insurance policy. The rate for one year is $.32 per $100.
   a. Find the cost for one year.
   b. Find the cost of a 5 year policy.

SECTION 2   Fire Insurance: Co-Insurance Clause

Class Drill

1. Find 80% of $15,000
2. Find 80% of $35,000
3. Find 80% of $29,000
4. Find 80% of $32,000

5. Divide $27,400 by 100
6. Divide $33,500 by 100
7. Find 3/4 of $4,800
8. Find 2/3 of $6,300

Sample Problem

Mr. Herman bought a house for $30,000. He purchased a $20,000 fire insurance policy. The policy contains an 80% co-insurance clause. If a fire caused damage to the house of $6,000, how much should the insurance company pay?

Explanation

In order to discourage people from buying very small fire insurance policies, insurance companies state in the policy that they will pay the full fire loss only if the owner insures at least a certain per cent of the value of the property. If the property is not insured for this percent, then the insurance company will pay only part of the loss, and the owner must pay the rest of the loss. Thus the owner becomes a co-insurer. In New York, policies contain an 80% co-insurance clause. If the owner insures his property for at least 80% of the value, the fire insurance company will pay the full loss, up to the amount of the policy. If he insures for less than 80%, the insurance company will pay only part of the loss.

In the sample problem, 80% of $30,000, or $24,000, is the amount of insurance that must be carried in order to collect the full fire loss up to the amount of the policy. Thus, if a fire caused a $10,000 damage, the insurance company would pay the full $10,000 if the owner had a $24,000 policy. If fire caused a $25,000 damage, the insurance company would only pay $24,000, the amount of the policy. If the person carried a $30,000 policy, then the insurance company would pay any loss, up to the value of the house.

If the insurance policy is less than 80%, then the insurance company pays part of the loss. It compares the amount of the policy with the amount of insurance that should have been carried to collect the full loss, as follows:

$$\frac{Amount\ of\ Policy}{Amount\ that\ Should\ be\ Carried} \quad or \quad \frac{Amount\ of\ Policy}{80\%\ of\ Value\ of\ Property}$$

This fraction is then applied to the fire loss in order to find the amount that the company will pay.

Sample Solution

$$\begin{array}{r} \$30,000 \text{ Value of House} \\ \times .80 \\ \hline 24,000.00 \text{ 80\% of Value} \end{array}$$

$$\frac{20,000}{24,000} \times 6,000 = \$5,000$$

In this case, the insurance company will pay only $5,000 even though the loss is $6,000. The owner must pay the rest of the loss.

Problems

1. Mr. Evans insured his $25,000 house for $15,000. If the insurance policy has an 80% co-insurance clause, and a fire caused a damage of $4,000, how much should the insurance company pay?

2. A fire insurance policy for $28,000 contained an 80% co-insurance clause. If the building was worth $40,000, and a fire caused damage of $8,000, how much should the insurance company pay?

3. In each of the following problems, find the amount that should be paid by the fire insurance company if there is an 80% co-insurance clause.

	Value of Property	Amount of Policy	Amount of Fire Loss
a.	$10,000	$10,000	$ 7,000
b.	10,000	8,500	6,000
c.	10,000	6,000	4,000
d.	10,000	7,000	2,000
e.	10,000	8,000	8,500
f.	10,000	9,000	9,300
g.	50,000	10,000	3,200
h.	20,000	8,000	3,560
i.	35,000	21,000	8,400
j.	25,000	18,000	3,500
k.	15,000	13,000	9,375
l.	15,000	14,000	15,000

SECTION 3   Auto Insurance: Bodily Injury Liability Insurance

Class Drill

1. Find 10% of $139
2. Find 10% of $96
3. Find 50% of $207
4. Find 50% of $258
5. Find 100% of $222
6. Find 150% of $276
7. Find 150% of $108
8. Find 100% of $91

Sample Problem

Bill is 22 years old, single, and drives his own car. How much will a $25,000/$50,000 bodily injury liability insurance policy cost him each year? Bill lives in Queens and has a safe driving record for the past 3 years.

Explanation

If a driver injures somebody with his automobile, the injured party may sue for damages. To protect himself in the event of such a damage suit, the owner of a car buys liability insurance (also known as bodily injury insurance) as part of an automobile insurance policy. If the injured party wins the damage suit, the insurance company will pay the amount of damages, up to the amount of the policy.

In New York State every owner of an automobile must carry a $10,000/ $20,000 liability insurance policy. This means that the insurance company will pay up to $10,000 for injury to one person or up to $20,000 for injuries to several persons. If the court awards the injured person a judgment greater

than $10,000, the owner of the car must pay the balance out of his own savings. In New York State every owner must also carry a $10,000/$20,000 liability insurance coverage against uninsured motorists, in case the owner is injured by another motorist who does not carry liability insurance.

The premium for a $10,000/$20,000 liability policy depends on several factors:

1. Who drives the car
2. Where the car is garaged
3. The purpose for which the car is used
4. The driving record of the driver

To illustrate how the premium is found, here is a typical table of rates (rates vary from year to year and company to company)

Automobile Insurance—$10,000/20,000 Bodily Injury Liab.						
	Class					
Location	1	9	2	3	4	5
Manhattan	126	139	151	233	290	170
Bronx	112	123	134	207	258	151
Brooklyn	120	132	144	222	276	162
Queens	90	104	117	194	258	131
Nassau	77	77	96	158	250	108
Richmond	65	65	88	133	211	91

Add 10% for 20/40; 13% for 25/50; 21% for 50/100; 28% for 100/300

Class 1 means: There is no male operator under 25 years of age, the automobile is not used for business, nor is it driven to or from work.

Class 9 means: Same as Class 1, but the automobile is driven to or from work a distance of less than 10 miles one way.

Class 2 means: Same as Class 1, but the auto is driven to or from work a distance of 10 or more miles one way.

Class 3 means: There are one or male operators under 25 years of age, and each is either married or not the owner or principal operator of the auto.

Class 4 means: There is an unmarried male operator under 25 years of age who is the owner or principal operator of the auto.

Class 5 means: There is no male operator under 25 years of age and the automobile is used for business.

91

The insurance company uses a system of points to lower the premium for a safe driver and raise it for other drivers. Here is a typical system of points:

a. Safe driver—no points assigned for the past 3 years. 10% discount.

b. Driver training credit—male operator under 25 successfully completed an approved driver education course.

c. Other drivers pay more than the rates in the table, as follows:

1. One point is assigned for each automobile accident resulting in damage to any property, including the driver's car, in excess of $100, or in bodily injury or death, or two or more accidents each of which resulted in damage of $100 or less. Add 10% to the rate.

2. Two points are assigned for driving at an excessive rate of speed, where an injury to person or damage to property results, or where violations cause suspension or revocation of license. Add 50% to the rate.

3. Three points are assigned for operating a motor vehicle while intoxicated, or while disabled by reason of the use of drugs, or leaving the scene of an accident without stopping to report, or criminal negligence. Add 100% to the rate.

4. Four points—accumulated as shown above. Add 150% to rate.

No points are assigned for an accident if it occurred while the auto was parked, or struck in the rear, or where the operator of the other vehicle was convicted of a moving traffic violation, or where the other person was responsible for the accident and paid damages.

Sample Solution

Bill is in Class 4 because he is an unmarried male operator under 25 years of age who is the owner of the car. His premium, according to the table, is $258 in Queens for a $10,000/$20,000 policy. For a 25/50 policy, add 13%; then, because he is a safe driver, deduct 10%.

$258 Cost of 10/20	$258.00 Cost of 10/20
×.13	33.54 Added for 25/50
774	291.54 Cost of 25/50
258	− 29.15 10% discount for safe driving
$33.54 Added for 25/50	$262.39 Premium for 25/50 policy for safe driver

Questions

1. Why does the insurance rate go up in large cities?

2. Why is the insurance rate higher for young unmarried men?

3. Why does the insurance rate go up when the car is used for business?

4. Why does the rate go up for a driver when the insurance company assigns points?

5. In which county are the rates lowest? Why?

6. Which type of driver pays the highest rates? Why?

7. In which class would the insurance company place these drivers:
   a) Mr. Jones, age 36, single, uses his car on week-ends only.
   b) Miss Smith, age 21, single, uses her car on week-ends and during her vacation.
   c) Mr. Brown, age 43, drives his car to work each day 6 miles from his home.
   d) Mr. Henry, age 29, drives his car to work 12 miles from his home.
   e) Mr. Perry, age 23, married, drives to work 7 miles from his home.
   f) Bill, age 18, single, drives his father's car on week-ends.
   g) Joe, age 19, single, drives his own car to school 4 miles from his home.
   h) Mr. Towers, age 28, uses his car for business purposes.

Problems

1. Mr. Jones, age 36, single, uses his car on week-ends only.
   a) Use the table to find the cost of $10,000/$20,000 liability insurance if Mr. Jones lives in Manhattan
   b) If Mr. Jones wants a 20/40 policy, what would the policy cost him?
   c) What would the 20/40 policy cost if Mr. Jones has 1 point assigned to him by the insurance company because of a poor driving record?

2. Miss Smith, age 21, single, uses her car on week-ends.
   a) Use the table to find the cost of $10,000/$20,000 liability insurance if Miss Smith lives in Brooklyn.
   b) If Miss Smith wants a 25/50 policy, what would the policy cost?
   c) What would the 25/50 policy cost if Miss Smith has no points assigned to her because of her safe driving record for three years and is entitled to a 10% discount?

3. Mr. Brown, age 43, drives his car to work 6 miles from his home.
   a) Use the table to find the cost of $10,000/$20,000 liability insurance if Mr. Brown lives in the Bronx.
   b) If Mr. Brown wants a 50/100 policy, what would it cost?
   c) If Brown has 2 points assigned to him for a poor driving record, what would the 50/100 policy cost?

4. Mr. Henry, age 29, drives his car to work 12 miles from his home.
   a) Use the table to find the cost of $10,000/$20,000 bodily injury insurance if Mr. Henry lives in Nassau County.
   b) If Mr. Henry wants a 100/300 policy, what would it cost?
   c) If Mr. Henry has no points assigned to him because of his safe driving record for three years, what would the 100/300 policy cost?

5. Find the premium for bodily injury insurance in each case:

	Location	Class	Amount of Insurance	Driving Record
a)	Richmond	2	10/20	0 points for three years
b)	Manhattan	4	10/20	2 points
c)	Queens	3	10/20	1 point
d)	Bronx	1	10/20	3 points
e)	Nassau	9	25/50	0 points for three years
f)	Brooklyn	5	50/100	1 point
g)	Queens	4	20/40	2 points
h)	Manhattan	3	100/300	0 points for three years
i)	Bronx	2	25/50	2 points
j)	Richmond	9	50/100	1 point

6. Mr. Stern has $10,000/$20,000 bodily injury insurance. In an accident he injured two people. The first person sued and was awarded $7,000 by the court; the other person sued and was awarded $15,000.
   a) How much will the insurance company pay the first person? The second person?
   b) How much will Mr. Stern have to pay out of his own savings?

7. Bill, age 24, single, uses his own car for pleasure only.
   a) Use the table to find the cost of $10,000/$20,000 liability insurance, if Bill lives in Brooklyn.
   b) When Bill becomes 25, what will the same insurance cost him, according to the table?

8. Mr. Porter, age 33, uses his car for business. He lives in Manhattan.
   a) Use the table to find the cost of $10,000/$20,000 bodily injury insurance.
   b) If Mr. Porter moves to Nassau County, what will the same insurance cost him?

SECTION 4

Class Drill

Auto Insurance: Property Damage Insurance

1. Find 10% of $139
2. Find 10% of $ 77
3. Find 50% of $108
4. Find 50% of $112
5. Find 150% of $75

6. Find 5% of $40
7. Find 5% of $68
8. Find 5% of $43
9. Find 10% of $137
10. Find 5% of $246

Sample Problem

Bill is 22 years old, single, and drives his own car. How much will a $10,000 property damage insurance policy cost him each year? He lives in Queens, and has a safe driving record for the past 3 years.

Explanation

If a driver damages another person's property, the other person may sue for damages. To protect himself from financial loss, the owner of a car buys property damage insurance as part of his automobile insurance policy.

In New York State, every owner of an automobile must carry a $5,000 property damage policy. (This is in addition to the $10,000/$20,000 bodily injury insurance he must carry, as explained in the previous lesson)

The premium for property damage insurance is based on the same factors as liability insurance (see previous lesson). To illustrate how the premium is found, here is a typical table of rates (rates vary from year to year and company to company).

Automobile Insurance—$5,000 Property Damage Class						
Location	1	9	2	3	4	5
Manhattan	39	43	47	72	90	53
Bronx	36	40	43	67	83	49
Brooklyn	36	40	43	67	83	49
Queens	32	37	42	69	83	46
Nassau	31	31	39	64	91	43
Richmond	28	28	38	57	91	39

Add 5% for $10,000 policy; 6% for $15,000; 7% for $20,000; 8% for $25,000; 13% for 50,000; 18% for $100,000.

Sample Solution

Bill is in Class 4 because he is an unmarried male operator under 25 years of age who is the owner of the car. (See classes, page 91.) His premium, according to the table, is $83 in Queens for a $5,000 policy. For a $10,000 policy, add 5%; then deduct 10% for a safe driving record:

$83.00   5000 Policy
  4.15   5% more

 87.15   Premium for $10,000 Policy
  8.72   10% discount for safe driving

$78.43   Premium for safe driver for $10,000 policy

Problems

1. Mr. Jones, age 36, single, uses his car on week-ends only.
   a. Use the table to find the cost of $5,000 property damage insurance if Mr. Jones lives in Manhattan.
   b. If Mr. Jones wants a $10,000 policy, what would it cost?
   c. What would the $10,000 policy cost if Mr. Jones has 1 point assigned to him by the insurance company because of a poor driving record?

2. Miss Smith, age 21, single, uses her car on week-ends.
   a. Use the table to find the cost of $5000 property damage insurance if Miss Smith lives in Brooklyn.
   b. If Miss Smith wants a $10,000 policy, what would it cost?
   c. What would the $10,000 policy cost if Miss Smith has no points assigned to her because of her safe driving record?

95

3. Find the premium for property damage insurance in each case:

	Location	Class	Amount of Insurance	Driving Record
a)	Richmond	2	$ 5,000	0 points for three years
b)	Manhattan	4	5,000	2 points
c)	Queens	3	15,000	1 point
d)	Bronx	1	20,000	3 points
e)	Nassau	9	25,000	0 points for three years
f)	Brooklyn	5	50,000	1 point

SECTION 5   Auto Insurance: Comprehensive; Collision

Class Drill

1. Find 10% of $134
2. Find 10% of $76
3. Find 5% of $120
4. Find 5% of $80

5. Find 50% of $68
6. Find 50% of $124
7. Find 100% of $143
8. Find 150% of $60

Sample Problem

Mr. Brown is concerned that his car may be stolen, or it may be damaged in an accident. In order to protect himself, he buys comprehensive insurance, with a $50 deductible clause, and collision insurance, with a $100 deductible clause. His car is now worth $2,500.

a. If the car is stolen, how much should the insurance company pay?

b. In case of an accident causing $300 of damages to his car, how much should the insurance company pay?

Explanation

Comprehensive automobile insurance is purchased to protect the owner from financial loss resulting from the theft of the auto, or from damage caused by fire, vandalism, hail or flood. The owner would be protected up to the actual value of the car at the time of the loss.

Collision insurance is purchased to protect the owner from financial loss resulting from damage to his own car caused by a collision.

Many insurance companies do not wish to bother with small claims, and therefore offer what is called a "*deductible clause*" in the policy. A $100 deductible clause means that the insurance company will deduct $100 from the financial loss before paying. These clauses may be included in comprehensive insurance or collision insurance. Because small claims are avoided, the premium is reduced when a deductible clause is included in the policy. Many automobile owners are willing to have this clause, therefore, to reduce the premium.

Sample Solution

a. $2,500 Value of Car
      50 Deductible
  $2,450 Paid by company

b. $300 Damage
    100 Deductible
  $200 Paid by company

PROBLEMS

1. Mr. Palmer owns a car worth $3,000. He has comprehensive and collision insurance, each with a $100 deductible clause.
   a. If a collision causes damages of $500 to his car, how much would the insurance company pay?
   b. If fire causes damages of $60 to his car, how much would the insurance company pay?

2. Mr. Stone owns a car worth $2,500. He has comprehensive and collision insurance, each with a $50 deductible clause.
   a. If a collision causes damages of $475 to his car, how much would the insurance company pay?
   b. If the car is stolen, how much would the insurance company pay?

3. Mr. Benny has 10000/20000 bodily injury liability insurance, $5,000 property damage insurance, comprehensive insurance with a $100 deductible clause, and no collision insurance. In an accident he injured two people. In the law suit the first person was awarded $12,000 and the second person $5000. He also caused damage to the other car amounting to $750, and to his own car amounting to $600.
   a. How much would the insurance company pay the first person? the second person?
   b. How much would Mr. Benny have to pay out of his own savings for the injuries to the two people?
   c. How much would the insurance company pay for damages to the other person's car?
   d. How much would the insurance company pay for damages to Mr. Benny's car?

4. Mr. Washington has 10000/20000 bodily injury, $5,000 property damage insurance, comprehensive insurance with a $100 deductible clause, and no collision insurance. In an accident he injured three persons. As a result of the court case, Mr. Adams was awarded $8000, Mr. Brown was awarded $13000, and Mr. Callahan was awarded $4000. Damage to Mr. Washington's car was $600; damage to the other car was $500.
   a. How much would the insurance company pay for injuries to the three persons?
   b. If only Mr. Adams and Mr. Brown won the case, how much would the insurance pay each man?
   c. How much would the insurance company pay for damages to the other car?
   d. How much would the insurance company pay for damages to Mr. Washington's car?

SECTION 6   Life Insurance

Class Drill

1. Divide $4,320 by 10
2. Divide $745 by 100
3. Divide $13,000 by 1,000
4. Divide $40,000 by 1,000

5. Multiply $27.88 by 5
6. Multiply $23.12 by 8
7. Multiply $32.29 by 6
8. Multiply $49.90 by 12

Sample Problem   Mr. Thomas is 25 years old. He would like to buy a $5,000 ordinary life insurance policy. What would be the annual cost of the policy?

Explanation   Many people buy a life insurance policy to provide financial protection for dependents in the event of death. The cost of the policy is called the *"premium,"* the person who will receive the money is called the *"beneficiary."* There are several types of life insurance that a person may buy. Here are some popular ones.

1. *Ordinary (whole life) Insurance*—Premiums are paid during the entire life of the insured person. Rates are relatively low because payments are made until the death of the insured.

2. *Limited payment policy*—Premiums are paid for a set number of years, such as 10 years or 20 years. At the end of this time, the insurance is fully paid up, and the person is insured without payment of additional premiums for the rest of his life. The cost of this type of insurance is higher than ordinary life because payments must be made over a shorter period of time.

3. *Endowment policy*—Premiums are paid for a set number of years, such as 20 or 30 years. At the end of this time the amount of insurance is paid to the insured person. Premiums are high, because the company must save money to pay the insurance at the end of the period.

4. *Term insurance*—This is purchased for a set number of years or for a particular purpose, such as during an airplane trip. The term may run for the few hours of the trip or for several years. When the term ends, the insurance expires. The premium is the lowest of any type of life insurance.

In order to find the cost of a life insurance policy, it is necessary to look at a premium table which shows the cost of a $1,000 policy. Rates vary from company to company. Here is a typical table of rates for men: (rates for women are lower because of average longer life).

Annual Premium Rate for $1,000 Life Insurance				
Age at Issue	10 year Term	Ordinary Whole Life	20 Payment Life	20 Year Endowment
15	8.18	12.50	21.50	43.25
20	8.33	14.75	24.14	44.56
25	8.58	17.08	26.28	44.72
30	8.96	19.20	29.16	45.17
35	10.00	23.12	32.29	45.82
40	12.13	26.76	36.22	47.65

Sample Solution   Premium at age 25 for ordinary life is $17.08. For a $5,000 policy, multiply by 5:

$17.08 Premium for $1,000 policy

×5

$85.40 Premium for $5,000 policy

98

Problems

1. Mr. Webster bought, at age 30, a $7,000 ordinary life policy. What was his annual premium?

2. Mr. Sellers bought a $6,000 20-payment life policy at age 25. What was his annual premium?

3. Bill wishes to buy a $10,000 life insurance policy at age 20. What will his annual premium be if he buys:
   a. a 10 year term policy
   b. an ordinary life policy
   c. a 20 payment life policy
   d. a 20 year endowment policy

4. Mr. Barry bought a $15,000 ordinary life policy at age 30.
   a. How much will the beneficiary collect if Mr. Barry dies at age 35?
   b. What did the insurance policy cost Mr. Barry during the five years that he lived?
   c. How much more did the beneficiary receive than the amount paid in?

5. John bought a $5,000 20-year endowment policy at age 20.
   a. What was the annual premium?
   b. How much did John pay during the 20 years he held the policy?
   c. Did John receive more or less than he paid in after 20 years? How much?
   d. How do you explain your answer to (c)?

6. Mr. Donovan bought a $9,000 ordinary life policy at age 40.
   a. What was the annual premium?
   b. If Mr. Donovan died after 3 years, how much would his beneficiary collect?
   c. How much did Mr. Donovan pay for the insurance during the 3 years he had the policy?

7. Suppose Mr. Donovan (see example 6) had bought a $9,000 20-year endowment policy at age 40.
   a. What would the annual premium be?
   b. If Mr. Donovan died after 3 years, how much did he pay for the insurance?
   c. How much would the beneficiary collect?
   d. Why did the endowment policy cost more?

8. Mr. Smith bought a $25,000 10-year term policy at age 35.
   a. What was the annual premium?
   b. What was the cost during the next 10 years?
   c. How much would the beneficiary receive if Mr. Smith died after 7 years?
   d. How much would the beneficiary receive if Mr. Smith did not renew the policy and died after 12 years?

SECTION 7   Review Problems

1. Mr. Samuels insured his home against fire loss. The insurance cost him $.47 per $100.
   a. If he bought a $20,000 policy, what would it cost him?
   b. If he bought a $21,500 policy, what would it cost him?

2. Mr. Sternberg insured his home against fire loss. He bought a $23,000 policy at a cost of $.38 per $100.
   a. Find the annual premium.
   b. If he had purchased a three year policy, what would it have cost? (See rates for more than one year on page 88.)
   c. If he had purchased a five year policy, what would it have cost?

3. Mr. Bacon has a $20,000 house. A fire caused $4,000 worth of damage. How much will the insurance company pay in each case below if there is an 80% co-insurance clause in the policy?
   a. $20,000 policy
   b. $17,000 policy
   c. $12,000 policy
   d. $2,000 policy

4. Mr. Zucker lives in Manhattan. He is 32 years old, owns his car, does not use it for business, and takes the subway to work. He wishes to buy a 25/50 automobile liability insurance policy. He is a safe driver, and has had a safe record for the past five years.
   a. Refer to the table on page 91 to find the cost of a $10,000/$20,000 policy.
   b. Find the cost of a 25/50 policy before allowing for his safe record.
   c. Find the cost of his 25/50 policy after allowing for his safe record.

5. Tom is 19 years old, single, and drives his own car. He lives in Nassau County and has 1 bad point against him.
   a. Refer to the table on page 95 to find the cost of a $5,000 property damage insurance policy.
   b. What would a $10,000 policy cost him, before allowing for the bad point?
   c. What would a $10,000 policy cost him, after allowing for the bad point?

6. Mr. Davis has comprehensive insurance on his car with a $50 deductible clause. If the car is worth $3,100, and is stolen, what would the insurance company pay?

7. Mr. Washington carries a 20/40 automobile liability insurance policy, a $5,000 property damage policy, and a comprehensive policy. He does not carry collision insurance. His car is worth $2,900.
   a. In an accident he injured several persons. The case went to court. Mr. Adams was awarded $22,000, and Mr. Brown was awarded $5,000. How much should the insurance company pay?
   b. Mr. Columbo was awarded $2,000 by the court for damages to his car. How much should Mr. Washington's insurance company pay?

c. Damages to Mr. Washington's car amounted to $600. How much should his insurance company pay?

d. The comprehensive policy contains a $100 deductible clause. If Mr. Washington's car had not been damaged, but was stolen, how much should the insurance company pay?

8. Mr. Charney bought a $12,000, 20 year endowment policy at age 35.
   a. Find the annual premium. (Refer to table on page 98.)
   b. If Mr. Charney died after three years, how much would the insurance company pay his beneficiary?

UNIT 7

Installment Buying

SECTION 1

Finding the Monthly Payment (No Sales Tax)

Class Drill

Divide:
1. $522 by 6
2. $344 by 8
3. $434 by 7
4. $1,740 by 12

5. $221 by 13
6. $560 by 16
7. $666 by 18
8. $1,200 by 24

Sample Problem

Mrs. Stevens bought a $200 television set on the installment plan. She agreed to pay a down payment of $23 at the time of the purchase, and to pay the balance, plus a finance charge of $15 over the next 12 months.
a. How much money does she need at the time of purchase?
b. How much must she pay each month?
c. What is the total cost of the TV set?

Explanation

If a person wishes to buy something without paying the entire purchase price at once, he may pay the price over a period of time. This is known as buying on the installment plan, because the purchase price is paid in installments. For the privilege, the buyer must pay an extra charge, which is called the finance charge.

On July 1, 1969 the new federal Consumer Credit Protection Act, known as the Truth in Lending Law, went into effect. This law requires that the agreement signed by the purchaser, known as the installment sales contract, must include certain items:

1. The cash price—the cost if bought for cash.

2. a) The cash down payment—the amount to be paid at the time of purchase.

   b) The trade-in—the down payment in property, if any.

3. The unpaid balance—the amount owed.

4. The finance charge—the extra cost of paying on the installment plan.

5. The deferred payment price—the total purchase price.

6. The annual percentage rate—the finance charge shown as an annual rate, so that the buyer can compare the costs of various sellers.

7. The payments—the number, amounts, due dates. If any payment is more than twice the amount of the regular payments, this must be called a balloon payment in the contract.

New York State sets a limit on the amount of the finance charge. When the unpaid balance is $500 or less, the charge may not be greater than $10 per $100 per year; when it is over $500, then the limit is $8 per $100 for the excess over $500 per year. There are separate limits that apply when an automobile is purchased.

Sample Solution

a. $23 Cash needed at time of purchase

b. $200 Cash Price $16 payment each month
    23 Down Payment   12)192
   177 Unpaid balance
    15 Finance charge
 $192 Total to be paid on installment plan

c. $200 Cash price
    15 Finance charge
 $215 Installment plan price

Questions

1. What advantages are there for the buyer in buying on the installment plan? What disadvantages are there?

2. What advantages are there for the seller in selling on the installment plan? What disadvantages are there?

3. Why should the buyer refuse to sign a contract that has blank spaces in it?

4. Why should the buyer obtain a copy of the contract?

5. What are the provisions of the federal Truth in Lending Law?

6. What will happen if the buyer does not pay his installments?

Problems

1. The installment price of a radio including the finance charge is $50. If there is no down payment, and the buyer may pay over the next 10 weeks, how much will the installment be each week? (omit sales tax)

104

2. The cost of a television set when bought on the installment plan, including the finance charge, is $288. If no down payment is required, what must be paid each month if the buyer may pay installments for 24 months? (omit sales tax).

3. The cash price of a refrigerator is $370.00 (no sales tax). If the buyer purchases the refrigerator on the installment plan, she must pay $35 down, and she may pay the balance, plus a finance charge of $25, over the next 12 months.
   a. How much money does she need at the time of purchase?
   b. If she buys on the installment plan, how much must she pay each month?
   c. What is the total cost of the refrigerator when bought on the installment plan?

4. A television set cost $370 if bought for cash (no sales tax). If bought on the installment plan, the purchaser must pay $40 down, and must pay the balance, plus a finance charge of $30, for the next 15 months.
   a. How much money is needed at the time of purchase if bought on the installment plan?
   b. How much must be paid each month?
   c. What is the total cost of the television set if bought on the installment plan?

5-10. In each of the following problems find:
   a. How much money would be needed at the time of buying the article on the installment plan (no sales tax).
   b. The amount of each installment.
   c. The total cost of the article if bought on the installment plan.

	Cash Price	Down Payment	Finance Charge	Number of Installments
5.	$575	$20	$75	18
6.	331	25	30	12
7.	400	30	35	15
8.	500	29	45	12
9.	400	50	34	12
10.	631	50	85	18

SECTION 2   Finding the Monthly Payment (With Sales Tax)

Class Drill

Divide:
1. $ 324 by 12
2. $ 396 by 12
3. $ 624 by 12
4. $1,020 by 12

Divide:
5. $ 954 by 18
6. $1,350 by 18
7. $1,080 by 24
8. $1,152 by 24

Sample Problem

Mrs. Stevens (see page 103) bought the $200 television set on the same terms ($23 down, balance plus $15 finance charge over next 12 months) in New York City, and must pay a sales tax.
a. How much money does she need at the time of purchase?
b. How much must she pay each month?
c. What is the total cost of the TV set?

Explanation

When an item is purchased subject to a sales tax, the tax is paid at once with the down payment. Once the tax has been paid, the amount of each installment is the same amount it would have been without a sales tax. The total price of the item would be more, however, because of the tax.

Sample Solution

a. $200   Cash Price $23 Down Payment
     $\times .07$ 14 Sales Tax
    $14.00   Sales tax $37 Cash needed at time of purchase

b. $200   Cash Price $16 payment each month
     23   Down payment   12)192
    177   Unpaid balance
     15   Finance charge
   $192   Total to be paid on installment plan

c. $200   Cash Price
     14   Sales tax
     15   Finance charge
   $229   Total cost on installment plan

Problems

1. A refrigerator costs $185 if bought for cash, plus New York City sales tax. If bought on the installment plan, the customer would have to pay $20 down, plus the sales tax. The balance due, plus a finance charge of $15, would be paid for the next 12 months.
   a. How much money would be needed at the time of purchase if bought on the installment plan?
   b. How much would be paid each month?
   c. What would be the total cost of the set on the installment plan?

2. A television set would cost $298 plus New York City sales tax if the customer paid cash. If bought on the installment plan the customer would have to make a down payment of $35 and would have to pay the sales tax at the same time. The balance due, plus a finance charge of $25, would be paid for the next 12 months.
   a. How much money would be needed at the time of purchase if bought on the installment plan?
   b. How much would be paid each month?
   c. How much would be the total cost of the set if bought on the installment plan?

3–5 In each of the following problems assume that the New York City sales tax must be paid at once, and that the purchaser bought the article on the installment plan.
  a. How much money would be needed at the time of purchase?
  b. What would be the amount of each installment?
  c. What would be the cost of each article?

	Cash Price	Down Payment	Finance Charge	Number of Installments
3.	$550	$55	$45	12
4.	$400	$28	$36	12
5.	$650	$33	$55	12

SECTION 3

Finding the Number of Payments

Class Drill

Divide:
1. $1,040 by 20
2. $1,044 by 58
3. $432 by 36
4. $540 by 45
5. $740 by 10

6. $300 by 10
7. $134.40 by 5.6
8. $581.25 by $38.75
9. $77.40 by 6.45
10. $180.00 by 7.5

Sample Problem

Mrs. Thompson bought a refrigerator on the installment plan. The cash price was $175 plus sales tax. The installment terms were $25 down, plus sales tax, and the balance plus a finance charge of $15, to be paid at the rate of $13 per month.
  a. How much money does she need at the time of the purchase?
  b. How many months will it take to complete payments?
  c. How much will the final payment be?

Explanation

As explained on page 103, the federal Truth in Lending Law requires that the number of payments, and the amount of each payment be shown in the contract. Frequently the final payment is not the same amount as the other payments, and the contract must show the amount of this final payment. Buyers should be careful not to accept a contract requiring a very large final payment, because they may be unable to make this payment and then the seller may repossess the purchased item. A payment much larger than the others is called a "balloon payment."

Sample Solution

a. $175 Cash Price
   ×.07
   ————
   $12.25 Sales Tax

$25.00 Down Payment
 12.25 Sales Tax
 ————
$37.25 Cash needed at time of purchase

b. $175 Cash Price (without tax)
   $\underline{25}$ Down Payment

   150 Unpaid balance
   $\underline{15}$ Finance charge

   $165 Total to be paid on the installment plan

$$\begin{array}{r} 12+ \\ 13)\overline{165} \\ \underline{13} \\ 35 \\ \underline{26} \\ 9 \end{array}$$ This means it will take 12 full payments and a smaller final payment or 13 payments.

c. $13 $165 Total to be paid
    $\underline{\times\,12}$ full payments $\underline{-156}$ Paid in 12 full payments

    $156 paid $\ \ 9 Final payment
                                  (Notice that this agrees with the
                                  remainder in the division)

Problems

1. The cash price of a radio is $180 (no sales tax). If bought on the install-ment plan, the down payment is $27, and the balance plus a finance charge of $15 is to be paid at the rate of $14 a month.
   a. How many months will it take to pay?
   b. What will the final payment be?

2. A television set costs $290 if bought for cash (no sales tax). If bought on the installment plan, the terms are $39 down and the balance, plus a finance charge of $25, must be paid at the rate of $23 a month.
   a. How many months will be required to make all payments?
   b. How much will the final payment be?

3. A washing machine sells for $250 if bought for cash, plus the New York City sales tax. If bought on the installment plan, the buyer must make a down payment of $15 and must pay the sales tax at once. The balance, plus a finance charge of $35, must be paid at the rate of $15 a month.
   a. How much cash would be needed at the time of purchase?
   b. How many payments will have to be made?
   c. How much is the final payment?

4. If bought for cash, a piano costs $600 plus New York City sales tax. On the installment plan, the buyer must pay the sales tax plus a down payment of $45, and he pays the balance, plus a finance charge of $75, at the rate of $35 a month.
   a. How much cash would be needed at once?
   b. How many payments must be made after the down payment?
   c. What is the amount of the final payment?

5-10 In each of the following problems find:
  a. The amount of cash needed at the time of purchase (including N.Y.C. sales tax).
  b. The number of payments to be made.
  c. The amount of the final payment.

	Cash Price	Down Payment	Finance Charge	Amount of Each Payment
5.	$240	$35	$ 20	$18
6.	370	30	30	30
7.	420	40	50	28
8.	585	25	75	35
9.	750	60	130	30
10.	475	50	120	15

11-13 REVIEW

In each of the following problems assume that the New York City sales tax must be paid at once, and that the purchaser bought the article on the installment plan.
  a. How much money would be needed at the time of purchase?
  b. What would be the amount of each installment?
  c. What would be the cost of each article?

	Cash Price	Down Payment	Finance Charge	Number of Installments
11.	$600	$27	$75	18
12.	400	22	54	18
13.	650	38	90	18

UNIT 8

Profit and Loss

| SECTION 1 | **Finding Selling Price and Percent of Profit on Cost** |

Class Drill

1. Find 10% of $328
2. Find 25% of $244
3. Find 50% of $186
4. Find 20% of $ 50
5. Find 32% of $146
6. Find 24% of $ 58
7. Find 18% of $127
8. Find 29% of $345

Sample Problems

1. Mr. Benson has a radio and TV store. In order to cover his expenses and make a profit, he has found that he must mark up the cost of each radio 40%. If a radio cost him $60, at what should he sell it?

2. Mr. Jordan, in another radio store, sells the same radio for $90. If it costs him $60, what markup percent did he use?

Explanation

Every store owner must pay certain expenses, such as rent, telephone expense, salaries, electricity. To meet these expenses, and to make a profit, he must mark up the merchandise that he sells. The percent that he uses is called the markup percent, and the amount that he adds to the cost to set the selling price is called the markup.

Sample Solutions

1.
$60 Cost	$60.00 Cost
×.40 Rate of markup	+24.00 Markup
$24.00 Markup	$84.00 Selling Price

111

2. $90.00 Selling Price
   -60.00 Cost
   _____
   $30.00 Markup

$$\frac{\$30 \text{ Markup}}{\$60 \text{ Cost}} = \frac{1}{2} = 50\% \text{ Rate of Markup}$$

Explanation

   When finding the rate of markup, it may be necessary to use long division. For example, if the cost were $55, and the markup $34, the rate would be found as follows, to the nearest whole percent.

$34 Markup
$55 Cost

$$\begin{array}{r} .618 \\ 55\overline{)34.000} \\ 33\ 0 \\ \hline 1\ 00 \\ 55 \\ \hline 450 \\ 440 \\ \hline \end{array}$$ equals .62 equals 62%

Problems

1. A watch cost a dealer $50. What should he sell it for if he uses a markup rate of 40%?

2. A retailer bought a TV set for $125. If he uses a markup rate of 60%, what should the selling price be?

3. In each of the following problems find the selling price:

Cost	Markup Rate
a. $ 75	50%
b. 125	20%
c. 250	35%
d. 140	45%

4. A watch cost a dealer $50. What markup rate did he use if he sells it for $75?

5. A retailer bought a TV set for $125. What rate of markup did he use if he sells the set for $175?

6. In each of the following problems find the rate of markup to the nearest whole percent.

Cost	Selling Price
a. $ 80	$100
b. 160	240
c. 120	192
d. 200	270
e. 60	70
f. 85	125
g. 146	215
h. 350	510

SECTION 2   Finding Profit and Percent on Sales

Class Drill

1. Find 34% of $125

2. Find 21% of $ 63

3. Find 19% of $ 87

4. Find 24% of $146

5. Change 3/8 to a percent (nearest whole %)   7. Change 7/15 to a percent

6. Change 5/9 to a percent   8. Change 8/17 to a percent

Sample Problem

During the year a businessman bought goods for $40,000 and sold them for $60,000. His expenses were $12,000. Find:

a. his gross profit and his net profit

b. percent gross profit on sales (to nearest whole percent)

c. percent net profit on sales (to nearest whole percent)

Explanation

As explained previously, each businessman must pay not only for the merchandise that he sells, but also the various expenses of the business, such as rent, telephone, salaries, etc. The profit that he makes *before* subtracting these expenses is called the "GROSS PROFIT." The profit he makes *after* subtracting the expenses is called the "NET PROFIT."

Businessmen often wish to know what part of each dollar taken in as a result of a sale is the cost of the merchandise, what part is the gross profit, what part represents the expense, and what part is the net profit. For example, 60¢ of each dollar may be the cost, 40¢ the gross profit, 30¢ the expenses and 10¢ the net profit. To find these figures, it becomes necessary to change figures to a fraction of the sales, and then to a percent of sales.

Sample Solution

a)
$60,000 Sales
 40,000 Cost of Sales
 20,000 Gross Profit
 12,000 Expenses
 $8,000 Net Profit

c) $\dfrac{8,000 \text{ Net Profit}}{60,000 \text{ Sales}} = \dfrac{8}{60} = \dfrac{2}{15} = 13\%$

Net Profit on Sales

$$\begin{array}{r} .133 = 13\% \\ 15\overline{)2.000} \\ 1\,5 \\ \overline{50} \\ 45 \\ \overline{50} \\ 45 \end{array}$$

b) $\dfrac{20,000 \text{ Gross Profit}}{60,000 \text{ Sales}} = \dfrac{1}{3} = 33\%$

Gross Profit on Sales

The 33% gross profit means that 33¢ of each sales dollar was gross profit. The 13% net profit means that 13¢ of each sales dollar was net profit. In the form of a dollar bill, money received as a result of a sale would be made up of the three items shown in the cartoon on page 114.

Problems

1. The sales of a local business amounted to $150,000. If the cost of the goods sold amounted to $100,000 and expenses totaled $40,000, find a) gross profit and net profit; b) percent gross profit on sales; c) percent net profit of sales (nearest whole percent).

2. Mr. Turner has a retail store. His sales for the year were $200,000. The merchandise that was sold cost Mr. Turner $150,000 and his expenses were $25,000. Find a) gross profit and net profit; b) percent gross profit of sales; c) percent net profit of sales (nearest whole percent).

3–8 In each of the following problems find a) gross profit and net profit; b) percent gross profit of sales; c) percent net profit of sales. Find percent to the nearest whole percent.

	Sales	Cost of Sales	Expenses
3.	$140,000	$ 80,000	$40,000
4.	300,000	220,000	50,000
5.	175,000	100,000	45,000
6.	260,000	190,000	60,000
7.	180,000	130,000	30,000
8.	240,000	190,000	30,000

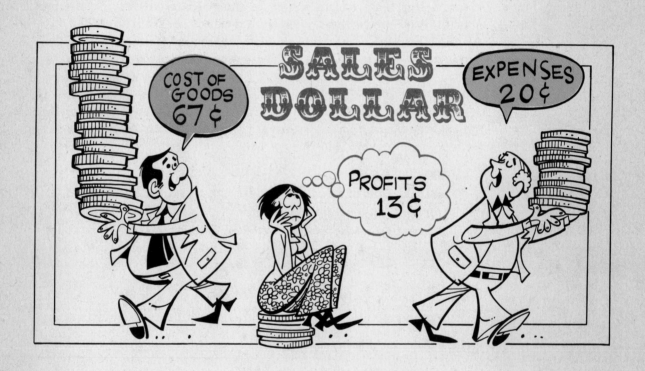

114

UNIT 9

Depreciation

Class Drill

Divide:
1. $4,900 by 8
2. $5,300 by 10
3. $2,250 by 9
4. $1,716 by 12

5. Find 10% of $2,455
6. Find 25% of $4,600
7. Find 15% of $2,100
8. Find 22% of $1,630

Sample Problem

Mr. Mathis paid $3,500 for a new car. He expects to keep it for 5 years, and then to sell it for $500. How much will the car depreciate each year?

Explanation

Many things that are used for several years, such as automobiles, machinery, furniture, gradually become worthless as the years go by. Some items are worth less because they gradually wear out; some become obsolete as new items are developed; most are worth less because time causes aging and deterioration. The decrease in value of these items is called "depreciation."

The value of the article when it is sold or discarded is known as the "scrap value." The total amount of depreciation over the life of the item may be found by subtracting the scrap value from the original cost.

When business firms list their expenses, such as rent, salaries, telephone, they also list depreciation of items that last more than a year. When the same amount of depreciation is taken each year it is known as the "straight-line" method of figuring depreciation.

Sample Solution

$3,500 Cost
  500 Scrap Value
$3,000 Total Depreciation

$600 Depreciation each year
5)$3,000

Problems

1. Mr. Brown bought a car for $3,000. He plans to keep it for 10 years, and to junk it without getting anything for it. How much is the yearly depreciation?

2. Mr. Tanner purchased an auto for $2,800. He expects to use the auto for 9 years, and then have it carted away without getting money for it. How much is the annual depreciation?

3. A business man bought machinery for $12,000. He expects to use it for 10 years, and to sell it at that time for $500. How much is the yearly depreciation?

4. A retailer bought a cash register for $450. He plans to use it for 5 years and then to sell it for $50. What is the annual depreciation?

5. Find the yearly depreciation in each case.

	Cost	Scrap Value	Estimated Life
a.	$4,500	$200	10 years
b.	2,000	700	3 years
c.	1,000	100	5 years
d.	2,500	50	6 years
e.	3,000	200	8 years
f.	2,700	100	5 years

6. The federal government permits a taxpayer in business to use a yearly rate of 10% to find depreciation on furniture. If he bought furniture for $590, how much depreciation could he take each year? How many years could he do this?

7. A business man may use a 25% rate of depreciation on his automobile. If the car cost $4,100, how much depreciation could he take each year? How long does he expect the car to last?

8. A business man uses a 20% rate of depreciation on his truck. If the truck cost $6,000:
a) How much is the annual depreciation?
b) What is the value of the truck at the end of the second

Review Problems Units VII, VIII, IX: Installment Buying, Profit and Loss, Depreciation

1. The installment price of a radio, including the finance charge, is $120. If a down payment of $30 is required, and the buyer must pay over the next 10 weeks, how much will the installment be each week? (no sales tax)

2. The cash price of a refrigerator is $413 (no sales tax). If the buyer purchases the refrigerator on the installment plan, she must pay $40 down, and must pay the balance, plus a finance charge of $35, over the next 12 months.

a. How much must she pay each month if she buys on the installment plan?

b. What is the total cost of the refrigerator when bought on the installment plan?

3. If bought for cash, a television set costs $358, plus the New York City sales tax. If bought on the installment plan, the customer must pay $40 down and must also pay the sales tax at once. The balance due, plus a finance charge of $30, must be paid over the next 12 months.

a. How much money would be needed at the time of purchase if bought on the installment plan?

b. How much would be paid each month?

c. How much would be the total cost of the set if bought on the installment plan?

4. The cash price of a radio is $220 (no sales tax). If bought on the installment plan, the terms are $30 down, and the balance, plus a finance charge of $15, must be paid at the rate of $16 a month.

a. How many months will be needed to complete all payments?

b. How much will the final payment be?

c. How much is the cost of the radio on the installment plan?

5. If bought for cash, a washing machine costs $375, plus the New York City sales tax. If bought on the installment plan, the buyer must pay the sales tax at once, plus a down payment of $50. The balance, plus a finance charge of $30, must be paid at the rate of $25 a month.

a. How much cash would be needed at the time of purchase?

b. How many payments would have to be made?

c. How much is the final payment?

d. What is the cost of the washing machine on the installment plan?

6. A retailer bought a suit for $75. What should he sell it for if he wishes a markup of 40%?

7. If a retailer bought golf clubs for $95 and sold them for $150, what was his percent markup on the cost to the nearest whole percent?

8. During last year, a firm's sales amounted to $134,500. The cost of the goods sold amounted to $95,000. The expenses totaled $17,400.

a. What was the gross profit?

b. What was the net profit?

9. The gross profit of a firm was $60,000, and the net profit was $45,000. If the sales totaled $120,000, find
   a. Percent gross profit on sales.
   b. Percent net profit on sales, to the nearest whole percent.

10. Mr. Brodsky bought a new car for $3,200. He plans to sell it after 5 years. He estimates that at that time it will have a scrap value of $500. How much is the annual depreciation?

UNIT 10

Stocks and Bonds

SECTION 1   Purchase of Stocks

Class Drill

Multiply
1. $37.00 × 100
2. $43.50 × 100
3. $81.75 × 100
4. $21.25 × 100

Multiply
5. $7\frac{1}{4}$ × 100
6. $52\frac{1}{2}$ × 100
7. $47\frac{1}{2}$ × 100
8. $29\frac{1}{4}$ × 100

Multiply
9. $ 8.50 × 35
10. $26.25 × 40
11. $38.50 × 56
12. $41.25 × 75

Sample Problem

Mr. Seymour bought 100 shares of General Motors stock at a price of $70\frac{1}{8}$. He paid the broker a commission of $61. What was the total cost of the stock?

Explanation

When a businessman wishes to assemble a large amount of money for a business, he may start a corporation and sell stock. Each share of stock represents part ownership of the corporation. A stock certificate is given to the buyer to show how many shares he owns. The price printed on the stock certificate is called the "par value."

Once shares of stock have been issued by the corporation, a person who wishes to buy shares must find another person who wishes to sell the shares he owns. In order to help find such a seller, there is a central place where representatives of the buyer and the seller meet. This place is called the "stock market" in the same way that a fruit market is a place where fruit is bought and sold.

When a person sells stock, his representative, called a stockbroker, tries to sell the stock at the highest price possible. The stockbroker of the buyer, on the other hand, tries to buy the stock at the lowest possible price. Many factors influence what this price will be: the profits of the corporation, the chances of increasing profits in the future, etc. When many persons wish to

sell their stock but only a few people wish to buy, the price of the stock will fall. When many persons wish to buy but not many wish to sell, the price will rise.

The broker charges a fee, or commission, for his services. Once the buyer and seller agree on a price, this price is reported on the stock ticker, so that people all over the country will know the most recent selling price of the stock. Prices are also reported in the daily newspaper, as shown below. The price at which stock is sold is called the "market price" of the stock.

New York Stock Exchange Transactions

Continued

1970 High.	Low.	Stocks and Div. In Dollars.	Sls. 100s.	First.	High.	Low.	Last.	Net Chge.
13⅝	10	Fansteel Inc	27	10¼	10⅜	9¾	9¾	— ½
18⅝	11¾	Far West Fin	31	12½	13¼	12⅜	12½	— ⅛
60	44	FarahMf .80b	44	46¾	47¾	46	46	—1
24⅜	15⅜	FAS Intl .47t	25	15	15	12¾	12¾	—2⅝
33½	25¼	Fedders .40	118	26⅛	27¼	26⅛	26¼	.....
27¼	23¼	FedMog 1.80	33	23⅜	24⅛	23⅛	23⅜	— ¼
15½	9¾	FedPac Elec	26	9¾	9⅞	9¾	9⅞	.....
19⅜	15½	F Pac pf1.26	1	15⅝	15⅝	15⅝	15⅝	+ ⅛
23⅞	19	FedPapBd 1	8	19⅞	20	19¾	19¾	— ⅛
22⅞	21⅛	F Pap pf1.15	Z⅛¼⅞?	¼¼¾	22¾	22⅛	22	+ ⅛
28⅜	19¾	FedSignS .60	8	20	20¼	19¼	19¼	— ¾
11⅝	7⅛	Federals Inc	32	7	7	6⅜	6⅜	— ⅞
39⅞	33	FedDeptStr 1	95	34	34¼	33⅝	33⅝	— ⅝
10⅞	8⅞	Fed Mtg Inv	59	9⅛	9⅛	8¾	8¾	— ½
25	16¾	Ferro Cp .70	24	16¾	16⅞	15½	15⅝	—1⅛
28¾	19	Fibrebrd .70	23	19⅝	20¾	19⅜	19⅞	— ⅛
29	23⅛	FieldctM 1.40	6	26	26½	26	26½	+ ½
39	30¾	Filtrol 2	9	30½	30½	30⅛	30½	— ½
23⅛	12⅞	Fin Federatn	119	13⅛	14⅛	12⅝	12⅞	.....
52⅝	37⅜	Firestne 1.60	49	37¾	37¾	36⅝	36⅞	— ½
42¾	27¾	Fst Chrt 2.29f	501	36½	36⅞	35¼	35¼	—1⅜
24½	19¾	Fst Mtge 1.44	111	19⅞	20⅛	19¾	19⅞	+ ⅛
74⅞	61¼	FstNCity 2.40	122	64	64⅜	63¼	63¼	—1½
34⅞	27	Fischbch .80	8	26⅝	27	26⅝	26⅝	— ⅜
19⅞	11⅝	Fishr Fd .05e	26	12¼	12⅜	12	12¼	+ ¼
15½	10¼	FisherScl .16	22	10⅛	10¼	9¾	9¾	— ½
13⅞	9¾	Fleming .50	12	10¼	10½	10⅛	10⅛	+ ⅛
26	21⅛	Flintkote 1	440	21⅞	22¼	21½	21½	— ⅞
36¼	29	Flint pfB2.25	3	32	32	32	32	—1
40¾	24½	Fla E Coast	42	23½	25⅜	23⅜	23¾	— ¾
22⅜	17⅞	Fla Gas .50	275	18⅝	18⅞	18¼	18½	—
52½	46	Fla Pow 1.60	39	47¼	48¼	47¼	47¼	— ¼

1970 High.	Low.	Stocks and Div. In Dollars	Sls. 100s.	First	High.	Low.	Last	Net Chge.
66⅝	53¼	IntFlaFr .50b	82	54¼	55¼	54	54	— ½
29	24⅝	Int Harv 1.80	80	25½	26	25½	25½	.....
19¼	15	IntHold 1.23e	6	15	15	14⅞	14⅞	— ⅛
43¾	15¼	Int Indust	127	15¾	16⅜	14¾	14¾	— ¾
56	24½	Int Ind pf1.70	14	24¾	24¾	24	24	—1
14⅝	10¾	Int Miner	370	11½	11½	10¾	11	— ½
17	12	Int Mng .10e	27	12⅜	13¼	12	12	— ⅜
46¾	39½	Int Nick 1.20	217	41	41½	40⅛	40⅜	— ⅞
40	32¼	Int Pap 1.50	250	33⅜	33⅝	33	33⅛	— ½
14⅛	8½	Intl Rectif	17	8¼	8¾	8¼	8¼	— ¼
4⅜	35	Int Salt 1.40	12	34¼	34¼	34	34¼	— ¾
60⅛	47¼	Int T&T 1.05	408	47¾	48⅞	46½	46½	— ⅞
197	159½	IntT&T pfD 4	z140	159½	159½	157	157	—2½
182	152½	IntT&T pfE 4	z10	143	143	143	143	—9½
112	94½	IntT&T pfH 4	1	93½	93½	93½	93½	—1
109½	91¼	ITT pfI 4.50	11	91¾	92	91¾	92	+ ¾
103	88	IntT&T pfJ 4	12	88	88	87	88	.....
99	84½	IntT&T pfK4	31	84	85	82¾	82¾	—1¾
27	21¼	Int Util 1.40	72	22¾	23¼	22¾	22⅞	+ ⅜
28⅝	22⅝	Int Util A	65	23⅜	23¾	23⅜	23⅜	+ ⅛
28½	21¾	IntUtil pf1.32	10	27	27	27	27	—1½
27½	21	Interpace 1	9	25⅜	25⅜	24¾	24¾	— ⅞
82½	74	Interpce pf 5	1	78¾	78¾	78¾	78¾	—1
18¾	14	Int Brand .90	12	14⅛	14¼	14	14	.....
28	16⅛	InterDStr .60	12	16⅛	16⅝	16⅛	16⅛	— ¼
18⅞	16¾	IntersPw 1.24	12	17½	17⅞	17½	17⅞	+ ⅛
37¾	29¼	Iowa Beef	58	30¾	31	29⅛	30⅞	+ ⅜
19¾	17¼	Ia El LP 1.30	13	18⅝	18⅞	18⅝	18¾	+ ⅛
22¾	20	Ia Ill GE 1.38	21	20⅛	20⅛	20	20	— ¼
28	24	IowaPLt 1.60	13	23⅞	23⅞	23¼	23¼	— ¾
22	19¾	IowaPSv 1.36	4	20	20	19⅞	19⅞	— ⅛
35½	23¼	Ipco Hosp .34	32	25½	25¾	24½	24½	—1¼
30¾	24¼	ITE Imp .60	46	26	26	24½	24¾	—1⅜
90¼	39¼	Itek Corp	422	42¾	44	40⅝	41¾	+ ¾
136¾	123	ITT Sv pf4.50	1	121¼	121¼	121¼	121¼	—1¾

1970 High.	Low.	Stocks and Div. In Dollars.	100s.	First.	High.	Low.	Last.	Net Chge.
47⅝	36	MobilOil 2.40	x238	40¾	41¼	40⅝	40¾	.....
30¼	24½	Mohasco 1.10	111	24⅜	24½	22⅜	22½	—2½
87	38¾	Mohwk Data	263	38⅞	41⅜	38⅞	39⅛	.....
25¼	19⅜	Monarch 1.20	26	18¾	18¾	18	18	—1⅜
25⅞	15⅜	Monogm Ind	70	16⅛	17	15½	15¾	— ⅜
25	19⅞	Mon RR .25g	6	20	20¼	20	20	.....
50⅜	32¾	MonroEq .60	127	32¾	33⅜	32½	32½	— ¼
37⅜	30½	Monsan 1.80	125	34⅛	35⅛	34⅛	34⅞	+ ¼
49	43½	Monsa pf2.75	3	44¼	44¼	44¼	44¼	.....
30¾	27¼	MontDUt 1.78	5	28⅜	28¾	28⅜	28¾	+ ⅜
31¾	26	Mont Pw 1.68	61	26⅝	26⅞	26½	26⅞	— ⅛
17½	10	Moo McCor	34	10¼	10½	10¼	10¼	.....
71	57	MorganJ 2.40	81	57¼	58½	57⅛	57⅜	— ⅝
30	24⅝	MorseSho .70	9	24½	24½	24¼	24¼	— ⅜
40	26	Mor-Nor .80	102	25¾	26⅜	25½	26	..
141¾	86	Motorola 1	169	88	90½	85¾	87	+ ¾
29¾	27¼	MtFuelS 1.80	4	28	28	27½	27½	— ¼
23½	21⅜	MtStaTT 1.36	9	21⅝	21⅝	21½	21½	.....
19⅛	14¾	MSL Ind .40	22	14⅝	14¾	14⅛	14⅛	— ¾
23⅜	19½	Munsingwr 1	21	21⅛	21⅛	20⅝	20¾	— ¾
27¾	22¾	Murphy 1.20	16	25½	25½	25¼	25¼	— ¼
11⅝	8⅝	Murphy Ind	16	9¼	9⅞	9⅛	9⅛	— ⅛
22½	17⅜	MurphOil .60	11	17¼	17⅜	16⅞	17⅛	— ¼
76	65¼	MurpO pf5.20	1	66	66	66	66	+ ¾
16⅝	13½	MurryOh .60	3	13⅞	13⅞	13¾	13¾	— ⅛
68½	42⅝	Nalco Ch .70	92	41	41	38¾	38¾	—4
40⅞	26¼	Narco Sci .60	11	26	26	24¾	25⅛	—1⅛
43⅜	28½	NashuaCp .44	24	28¾	28⅞	27⅝	28¼	— ¼
24¾	15⅝	Nat Airlin .40	163	15¾	16¼	15⅝	16¼	+ ½
26⅞	19½	N Aviat 1.24e	38	19	19⅜	19	19⅛	— ⅜
55	48⅜	Nat Bisc 2.20	43	49⅛	50	49⅛	49¼	+ ⅛
75¼	56	Nat Can .80	44	56	56	54	54	—2
67	50¼	N Can pf 1.50	20	50¾	50¾	48	48	—2¼
171¾	115¾	NatCash 1.20	222	115½	120½	115	115	—2½
61	61	Nat Cash wi	1	59	59	59	59	—2

Numbers shown represent dollars. For example, a price of 35 means stock was sold for \$35 per share. Instead of showing cents, prices are shown as eighths of a dollar—1/8, 2/8 or 1/4, 3/8, 4/8 or 1/2, 5/8, 6/8 or 3/4, 7/8. It is important to memorize the number of cents these fractions represent in order to work with the fractions more easily.

In order to learn how to read the stock exchange page, let us take the stock of Fedders Corp. as an example. The first two columns at the left show the highest selling price and the lowest selling price during the current year. For Fedders Corp. the highest price was $33\frac{1}{2}$, the lowest price was $25\frac{1}{4}$. The next column after the name of the stock tells how many hundred shares were sold during the day. For Fedders, 118 hundred shares, or 11,800 shares were sold during the day. The next four columns tell what happened to the price of the stock during the day. The price of the first sale was $26\frac{1}{8}$; the highest selling price during the day was $27\frac{1}{4}$; the lowest selling price during the day was $26\frac{1}{8}$; the final selling price at the end of the day was $26\frac{1}{4}$. The last column shows how the closing price compares with the closing price reported the previous day. In this case there was no change from the closing price of the previous day.

Price 70⅛ means $70.12½
$70.12½ or $70.125 for one share
$70.125 × 100 shares = $7,012.50 for 100 shares
　　　　　　　　　　 61.00 Commission
　　　　　　　　 $7,073.50 Cost of 100 shares

Notes

1/8 = .12½ or .125	5/8 = .62½ or .625
2/8 = 1/4 = .25	6/8 = 3/4 = .75
3/8 = .37½ or .375	7/8 = .87½ or .875
4/8 = 1/2 = .50	

Remember: To multiply by 100, move the decimal point 2 places to the right.

Questions

These questions are based on the newspaper clipping shown on page 120. Write each answer in two forms: first, as shown in the newspaper; second, as dollars and cents. For example; the answer to 1a is 36-7/8, or $36.87½.

1. Look at the line for Firestone Corporation.
    a. What was the closing price at the end of the day?
    b. How high did the price go during the day?
    c. What was the lowest price paid during the day?
    d. What was the highest price paid during the year?
    e. What was the lowest price for the year?
    f. Was the closing price higher or lower than the closing price of the previous day? By how much?
    g. How many shares were sold during the day?

2. Look at the line for International Harvester Corp. Answer questions a to g above.

3. Answer questions a to g above for Motorola Corp.

4. Answer questions a to g above for Mobil Oil Corp.

Problems

1. Find the cost of 100 shares of each of the following stocks if bought at the closing price, as shown in the newspaper clipping on page 120, before paying commission to the broker.
    a. Mor-Nor Corp.　　d. Far West Finance　　g. Ferro Corp.
    b. Monarch Corp.　　e. FAS International　　h. Firestone Corp.
    c. Fansteel Inc.　　　f. Fedders Corp.　　　i. International Paper

2. Mr. Benson bought 100 shares of National Biscuit Corp. at 49¼. If he paid his broker a commission of $58, what was the total cost of the stock?

3. Mr. Hoffman bought 100 shares of Gillette Corp. at $40\frac{1}{8}$. If he paid his broker a commission of $54, what was the total cost of this stock?

4. Find the cost including commission, of each of the following purchases of stock:

Stock	No. of Shares	Price per Share	Commission
a. Ford Motor	100	$41\frac{3}{4}$	$54
b. Gerber	100	$34\frac{5}{8}$	51
c. Gimbel Bros.	100	$35\frac{3}{8}$	52
d. Goodyear	100	$22\frac{7}{8}$	45
e. National Steel	50	38	41
f. General Tire	25	$16\frac{1}{4}$	26

5. EXTRA CREDIT—Obtain a copy of a daily newspaper that has New York Stock Exchange quotations shown. Ask your teacher for the date he wishes to use. Look up closing prices for the stocks listed in problem 1. Which stocks have gone up in price? Which ones have dropped in price? Find the cost of 100 shares of each stock at current prices.

SECTION 2   Sale of Stocks

Class Drill

Multiply:

1. $27\frac{1}{2}$ × 100
2. $43\frac{1}{4}$ × 100
3. $21\frac{3}{4}$ × 100
4. $ 9\frac{1}{8}$ × 100
5. $32\frac{3}{8}$ × 100
6. $14\frac{5}{8}$ × 100
7. $29\frac{1}{4}$ × 100
8. $32\frac{7}{8}$ × 100
9. $76\frac{3}{4}$ × 100
10. $83\frac{1}{2}$ × 100
11. $123\frac{3}{8}$ × 100
12. $79\frac{5}{8}$ × 100

Sample Problem

Mr. Norton bought 100 shares of General Electric stock at $69\frac{5}{8}$, and paid the broker a commission of $60. Several years later he sold the stock at $74\frac{1}{4}$, and paid a commission of $61. He also had to pay a state transfer tax of $5.00. Find Mr. Norton's profit on the sale of stock.

Explanation

When a person sells his stock, he must pay the broker a fee for his services, just as he had to pay for the services when he bought the stock. In addition, he must pay a tax, known as the transfer tax, whenever he sells his stock. Both the broker's commission, and the transfer tax are deducted from the selling price of the stock before the balance is turned over to the person selling his stock.

To find the profit on the sale, find the cost of the stock, then find the amount received from the sale, and find the difference. If the seller receives more than he paid for the stock, he has made a profit; if not, he has a loss.

$$\underline{Cost}$$

$69\frac{5}{8} = \$69.625$

$69.625 \times 100 = \$6,962.50$ Cost

$\underline{60.00}$ Commission

$\$7,022.50$ Total Paid

$$\underline{Selling\ Price}$$

$74\frac{1}{4} = \$74.25$

$74.25 \times 100 = \$7,425.00$ Selling Price

Less Com. 61

Tax $\underline{5}$

Deduction $\underline{66.00}$

$\$7,359.00$ Cash received

$\$7,359.00$ Cash Received

$\underline{7,022.50}$ Cash Paid

$\$336.50$ Profit on Sale

Problems

1. Mr. Abrams sold 100 shares of his Northwest Airlines stock at 20. He paid the broker a commission of $42, and paid a transfer tax of $5. How much cash did Mr. Abrams receive as a result of the sale?

2. Mr. O'Connor sold 100 shares of General Telephone at 26. He paid the broker a commission of $47, and paid the transfer tax of $5. How much cash did he receive?

3. Find the cash received in each of the following sales of stock:

Stock	No. of Shares	Price per Share	Commission	Tax
a. Ford Motor	100	$45\frac{1}{4}$	$56	$5
b. Gerber	100	$39\frac{3}{8}$	53	5
c. Gimbel Bros.	100	$21\frac{1}{8}$	43	5
d. Goodyear	100	$19\frac{7}{8}$	41	5

4. Mr. Hanson bought 100 shares of American Telephone at 50, and paid a commission of $59. Some time later, he sold the stock at 60, paid a commission of $60 to his broker, and paid $5 in transfer taxes.
   a. What was the total cost of the stock?
   b. How much cash did Mr. Hanson receive when he sold the stock?
   c. How much was the profit or loss?

5. Mr. Napoli bought 100 shares of RCA at 31, and paid a commission of $49. He sold the stock at 34, paid a commission of $51, and transfer tax of $5.
   a. How much did he pay for the stock, with commission?
   b. How much cash did he receive when he sold the stock?
   c. What was the profit or loss?

6-9 In each problem find:
  a. cash paid when purchased
  b. the cash received when sold
  c. profit or loss on the sale

	No. of Shares	Cost per Share	Com. on Purch.	Sale Price per Share	Com. on Sale	Tax on Sale
6.	100	$32\frac{1}{2}$	$50	$34\frac{1}{4}$	$51	$5
7.	100	$15\frac{3}{8}$	37	$18\frac{1}{2}$	40	5
8.	100	$28\frac{5}{8}$	48	$26\frac{7}{8}$	47	5
9.	100	$41\frac{1}{4}$	54	$41\frac{1}{4}$	54	5

SECTION 3   Finding the Dividend and Yield

Class Drill

Multiply:
1. $ .80 × 100
2. $1.25 × 100
3. $ .74 × 100
4. $2.32 × 100

Divide:
5. 80 by 2,000
6. 150 by 3,000
7. 30 by 500
8. 125 by 2,500

Sample Problem

Mr. Seymour owns 100 shares of Mobil Oil Corp. stock, which cost him $3775. Last year he received dividends of $2.40 a share.
a) How much did he receive?
b) What percent did he earn on his investment?

Explanation

On page 119 we learned that a stockholder is a part owner of a corporation. When a corporation makes profit, part of the profit may be distributed to the owners—the stockholders. This distribution of profit is called a "*dividend.*" The amount of the dividend, if any, is decided upon by the Board of Directors, which is elected by the stockholders. Usually some of the profits are kept in the business to permit the corporation to grow, and some of the profits are distributed to the owners.

If you look at the New York Stock Exchange page shown on page 120, you will notice a number written after the name of many corporations. This number shows the amount of the annual dividend paid. For example, Fedders Corp. pays a dividend of $.40 per year on each share of stock. Dividends usually are paid four times a year—quarterly.

A stockholder likes to know, in addition to the amount of dividends he receives during the year, what percent he earned on his investment. In this way, he can compare his earnings in stock with other possible earnings—such as in the savings bank. To find the percent or "*yield,*" as it is called, divide the dividend by the cost of the stock, and change the decimal to a percent. Divide to four decimal places in order to find the answer to the nearest tenth of a percent.

a) $2.40 a share × 100 shares = $240.00 Dividends for year

b) $\dfrac{240 \text{ Dividends}}{\$3,775 \text{ Cost}}$ = 3,775)$\overline{240.0000}$ .0635 = .064 = 6.4% (Rate on Investment nearest tenth %)

226 50

13 500
11 325

2 1750
1 8875

Refer to the newspaper clipping on page 120.

1. How much per share does Firestone pay in dividends?

2. How much does International Nickel pay per share?

3. Extra credit: What does a letter written after the amount of the dividend mean? Look at the footnotes in the newspaper on the page showing N.Y. Stock Exchange.

1. Mr. O'Brien received $125 in dividends last year on stock which cost him $2,500. What rate did he earn on his investment?

2. Mr. Caligeri received dividends of $70 last year on stock which cost him $1,750. What percent did he earn on his investment?

3. Mr. Gordon owns 100 shares of International Harvester stock, which pays a dividend of $.45 per share each quarter. (a) How much were his dividends for the year? (b) If the stock cost Mr. Gordon $3,600, what was the annual rate of return on his investment?

4. Henry Klein owns 100 shares of Motorola stock, paying a dividend of $.25 per share quarterly. (a) How much did he earn for the year? (b) if the stock cost him $10,000, what was his rate of return?

5. In each of the following problems, find the rate of return earned on the investment, to the nearest tenth percent:

	Dividend for Year	Cost of Stock
a)	$ 65	$2,340
b)	125	3,540
d)	230	3,345
d)	140	2,575
e)	176	2,300
f)	145	2,780

6. Look at the dividends and closing prices of the following stocks shown on page 120. What rate of return does each stock pay to investors? (Find answers to the nearest tenth of a percent).

a. National Cash Register   f. Fedders Corp.
b. Monarch Corp.   g. International Nickel
c. Motorola Corp.   h. International Paper
d. National Can   i. International Salt
e. Filtrol   j. Munsingwear Corp.

SECTION 4   Buying and Selling Bonds

Multiply by 10:

1. $ 95   6. 101\frac{3}{4}$

2. $ 86   7. $ 98$\frac{1}{8}$

3. $102   8. $ 96$\frac{3}{8}$

4. $ 75$\frac{1}{2}$ 9. $ 87$\frac{5}{8}$

5. $ 86$\frac{1}{4}$ 10. $ 92$\frac{7}{8}$

Sample Problem

Mr. Howard bought 5 Alcoa 6% bonds at a price of $81. He paid a commission of $12.50 to his broker.

a. Find the cost of the bonds.

b. How much income will Mr. Howard receive from the bonds each year?

Explanation

When a corporation wishes to borrow money for a long period of time, it issues "bonds." Bonds are promises to pay money that was borrowed when the bonds were issued. The corporation agrees to pay a certain rate of interest for the borrowed money, and agrees to pay the money back at a specific date. Corporate bonds are usually issued for $1,000 each. This amount is printed on the bond certificate, and is known as the par value of the bond.

Bonds are bought and sold in a manner similar to stocks. When a person wishes to buy a bond that was previously issued, he must find a person who owns some bonds and wishes to sell them. Once again, the stock exchange is used as a central place where representatives of the buyer and seller meet, as explained on page 119. The buyer's broker tries to buy the bonds at the lowest possible price, while the seller's broker tries to sell the bonds at the highest possible price. Many factors influence what the price will be: the absolute assurance that the corporation will be able to pay the bonds when they are due; current interest rates compared with the interest rate on the bond, etc. For example, if the interest rate on a bond issued several years ago is 4%, and new bonds pay 8%, buyers will not be willing to pay the par value of the 4% bond. As a result, the seller will be forced to sell the bond at a much lower price, or he will not be able to sell the bond at all.

When the buyer and seller agree on a price, this price is reported to the public, so that people will know the most recent selling price of bonds. Prices are reported in the daily newspaper, as shown below. The selling price of a bond is called the "market price."

Numbers shown represent a percent of the par value of the bond. For example, a price of 87 means 87% of a $1000 par value, or a market value of $870. A simple way of changing the price to a dollar value is to multiply by 10. In this case, 87 × 10 equals $870. As in the case of stock, prices are shown in eighths. A price of 92$\frac{1}{8}$ would mean that a $1000 bond would cost $921.25, because 1/8 equals $.125, and $92.125 × 10 = $921.25.

To read the bond prices, let us use General Electric bonds as an example. (See center column) The columns are similar to the columns showing stock prices, because they show high and low prices for the year ($79\frac{1}{2}$, $72\frac{1}{4}$), and prices for the day ($76\frac{1}{4}$ high, $75\frac{3}{8}$ low, and $75\frac{3}{8}$ close). After the name of the bond, it shows "5.30s 92." This means an interest rate of 5.30%, and the bonds must be paid in 1992. The sales column shows that 22 $1,000 bonds were sold during the day. The interest rate is always applied to the par value of the bond to find the amount of interest.

New York Stock Exchange Bond Trading

CORPORATION BONDS

1970 High.	Low.		Sales in $1,000.	High.	Low.	Last.	Net Chge.
		A—B—C—D					
74	64	Air Red cv3⅞s87	10	67	67	67	— ½
79⅛	74½	Allegh L cv4s81	9	75	75	75	.....
88	82⅛	Allied Ch 6.60s93	61	83¾	83	83½	+ ½
76⅜	68⅝	Allied Ch 5.20s91	20	71¾	71¾	71¾	—1
77¼	73⅞	Allied Ch 3½s78	5	76¼	76¼	76¼	.....
78¾	75	Allied Prod 7s84	7	75½	75¼	75½	— ¼
112	87	Allied St cv4½s81	15	89½	89½	89½	—4
80	66	Allied Str cv4½s92	73	75½	74	74	—1½
85½	75½	AlliedSup cv5¾s87	4	75¾	75½	75¾	+ ¼
83¾	78⅝	Alcoa 6s92	8	81	79	81	+2
102	85	Alcoa cv5¼s91	28	88	86½	86½	—1½
75½	70	Alum Can 4½s80	10	71	71	71	.....
109⅜	90	AAir Filt cv6s90	10	96¾	96¼	96¾	+ ¾
175	111	AAirFilt cv4⅞s87	16	121	120	120	+4
109½	93⅝	AmAirlin cv5½s91	104	94	93⅛	93⅜	—2⅝
79½	63	AmAirlin cv4¼s92	112	65¼	64½	64½	— ½
101½	86½	Am Airlin cv4s90	10	88	87½	88	+ ½
78½	72½	Am Brands 5⅞s92	8	73½	73	73	.....
69	66⅞	Am Brands 4⅝s90	5	67⅜	67⅜	67⅜	.....
94	78	Am Bdcst cv5s93	17	78	75¼	78	.....
84⅛	76¼	Am Can 6s97	1	82⅛	82⅛	82⅛	— ⅛
59	56	Am Can 3¾s88	8	60	60	60	+1½
73	66	Am Dist cv4⅜s86	25	66½	65	66	...
105½	93½	AmEnka cv5¼s94	11	102	102	102	.....
62	52	AmExprt cv5¼s93	65	52¼	52	52	— ⅛
61½	56¼	Am FP 5s2030	1	57	57	57	+ ½
97½	78⅞	Am Hoist cv4¾s92	3	83	83	83	—3½
69	63⅝	AmMFdy cv4¼s81	2	67½	67½	67½	+ ⅜
73½	68	Am Smelt 4⅝s88	2	68⅝	68⅝	68⅝	.....
69	63½	Am Sug 5.30s93	1	67⅛	67⅛	67⅛	—1⅜
.....	.....	AmSug 5.30s93reg	4	68½	68½	68½	.....
125½	118¼	ATT 8¾s2000ww wi	300	118½	118	118¼	— ⅞
100⅞	98¾	ATT 8¾s2000xw wi	3917	98¾	98¼	98¼	— ½
72¼	67	Am T&T 4⅜s85	46	69	68⅜	68⅜	— ⅝
.....	.....	AmT&T 4⅜s85reg	17	68½	68⅛	68½	.....
66½	59	Am T&T 3⅞s90	20	60⅛	60	60	— ¼
87¾	84	Am T&T 3⅜s73	55	87	86½	86¾	+ ¼
64⅛	58½	Am T&T 3¼s84	5	62	62	62	.....
59	54	Am T&T 2⅞s87	5	57	57	57	+2⅛
97	94	Am T&T 2¾s71	34	96 15-32	96¼	96⅜	—3-32
78¾	75⅞	Am T&T 2¾s75	152	78⅝	77¾	77¾	— ¾
67¼	62	Am T&T 2¾s80	25	65	64	65	...
[illegible]	53	Am T&T 2⅝s86	7	55	55	55	.....

MONDAY, APRIL 27, 1970

	U.S. Govt. Bonds	Other Dom. Bonds	Foreign Bonds	Total All Bonds
Day's sales..	......	a$18,150,000	$200,000	$18,350,000
Friday	......	a16,250,000	30,000	16,280,000
Year to date	......	a1,153,579,000	8,101,000	1,161,680,000
1969	......	a1,184,159,000	10,493,500	1,194,652,500

a—Includes International Bank Bonds

BOND ISSUES TRADED

	Issues	Advances	Declines	New Highs	New Lows
Yesterday	450	96	246	8	79
April 24	441	109	229	8	80
April 23	444	86	247	13	75

1970 High.	Low.		Sales in $1,000.	High.	Low.	Last.	Net Chge.
140½	106½	Eckrd Jack 4¾s88	14	107½	106½	106½	—1
64	50	EG&G cv3½s87	25	51⅛	50	50	—1
99	87	El PasoNG cv6s93	15	91	90	90	—1
102	86¼	EvansPd cv6¼s94	20	89	88⅛	89	+1
65	50	Fair Hill cv4⅜s92	23	53	50	50	—3
105¾	99½	Fam Fin 9½s89	15	100	99½	99½	— ½
94½	78½	Fibrebd cv4¾s93	4	80¼	80¼	80¼	+ ¾
103	96	Fst Mtge cv6¾s85	4	93	93	93	—3
85	81⅛	Fly Tiger 6.60s80	4	85	85	85	.....
76	65	FMC Cp cv4¼s92	29	65	64½	64¾	— ¼
70½	67	Food Fair 4s79	8	68⅛	68⅛	68⅛	.....
103½	100⅛	Ford Mot 8¼s74	184	101⅛	100½	101	+ ⅞
102⅜	97¼	Ford Mot 8⅛s90	25	98¼	97¾	97¾	+ ½
115½	96	ForMcKess cv6s94	5	96	96	96	.....
78	74¾	Fruehauf Cp 6s87	1	75	75	75	.....
99¾	81¾	Fruehauf cv5½s94	39	81	80	81	—1
124	87⅝	GAC Cp cv5⅞s94	62	90½	87	87	—3
106	102½	Gen Accept 9½s74	26	103½	102½	103	+ ½
79½	72¼	Gen Elec 5.30s92	22	76¼	75⅜	75⅜	— ⅛
58½	49½	Gen Host 6s90f	9	55½	55½	55½	+1¼
71	58	GenInst cv5s92	45	57½	57½	57½	—1
93½	88	GMot Acc 7⅛s90	20	89¾	88½	88½	—1½
85¾	77⅜	GMot Acc 6¼s88	30	81½	81	81⅛	— ⅜
83⅞	79	GMot Acc 5s77	62	82¼	82	82	—1¼
79⅞	74½	GMot Acc 5s80	35	76⅞	76	76⅞	+1⅝
79½	72½	GMot Acc 5s81	5	75⅜	75⅜	75⅜	+ ⅜
72	67¼	GMot Acc 4⅝s82	5	70	70	70	.....
69½	63⅛	GMot Acc 4⅝s86	20	66⅛	65½	66	— ¼
69	63	GMot Acc 4½s85	7	66¼	65¼	66¼	+3

1970 High.	Low.		Sales in $1,000.	High.	Low.	Last.	Net Chge.
97½	94¾	Pac G&E 3s70	4	97½	97¼	97½	+ ¼
83½	80	Pac G&E 3s74	3	82	82	82	—1
101½	99¼	PacT&T 8.65s2005	211	99⅝	99¼	99¼	.....
69	62¾	Pac T&T 4⅜s88	7	66⅛	66	66	.....
67⅝	57	PanAmA cv5¼s89	50	57	56	57	.....
189	133	PanAmA cv4⅞s79	16	133¼	133	133¼	+ ¼
102½	77	PanAmA cv4½s84	29	78	73	73	—4
59⅞	46	PanAmA cv4½s86	95	48	46½	47¾	+ ½
80	68½	Penn Dixie cv5s82	47	74	72	72	— ¼
112¼	100⅝	Penney cv4¼s93	5	103¾	103¾	103¾	— ¼
112¼	106¾	Pennan Co 9s94	5	105	105	105	—1¾
64½	61	Penn RR 4¼s81	2	63½	63½	63½	.....
105	100¾	Pennz Unit 9⅜s76	55	103⅛	103	103⅛	+ ⅝
93	84⅞	Pennz Unit 7½s88	21	85¾	85¾	85¾	— ¾
104¼	101	Phila El 9s95	289	101¼	101¼	101¼	.....
105½	100	Phila El 8s75	84	100¾	100	100¾	— ⅛
89	81⅛	Phila El 6½s93	15	86	85⅞	85⅞	— ⅛
84½	78¾	Phila El 6⅛s97	6	81	81	81	—1
68⅝	63	Phila Elec 4½s94	5	63	63	63	.....
94¼	89⅝	Phila El 2¾s71	6	94	93⅝	93⅝	— ⅜
136½	113¼	Philip Mor cv6s94	94	114¼	113	113	—1½
81½	78½	PitCC & StL 5s75	2	79⅛	79⅛	79⅛	+ ⅝
72	70½	PitCC& StL 3⅜s75	4	70	70	70	— ½
82½	77¼	Pub SEG 4⅝s77	11	81½	81½	81½	+ ½
85	65	Purex Cp cv4⅞s94	4	65⅞	65⅞	65⅞	+ ⅛
		Q—R—S—T					
79½	64½	RCA cv4½s92	42	66¼	65½	65¾	+ ¼
116½	102½	RalstPur cv4⅞s92	2	103½	103½	103½	.....
70⅞	62½	Rapid Am 7s94	115	66	61½	63	—3¾
37½	37¼	Reading 3⅛s95	4	37⅛	36½	36½	— ⅞
99½	75½	RedgBat cv5½s88	2	74	74	74	—1½
86	75	ReveCop cv5½s92	1	75⅛	75⅛	75⅛	— ⅞
76¾	65½	ReynMet cv4½s91	19	71¼	71	71	.....
103⅝	96½	Reyn Tob 8⅛s74	31	100	99¾	99⅞	+ ⅜
100½	89½	Reyn Tob 7⅞s94	10	96⅞	96⅞	96⅞	.....
85½	83	Reyn Tob 3s73	1	85½	85½	85½	.....
114¾	96½	Rheingld cv6½s94	7	100	100	100	— ⅛
54	49	StL SF 4s 97	2	52	52	52	.....
63	62	St L Sw 2nd 4s89	2	63	63	63	+1
73½	54½	SandersAs cv5s92	30	53½	53½	53½	—1¼
96¼	86	SaFeInd cv6¼s98	12	90	89¼	89¼	— ¾
106½	79	SaFeInt cv5½s87	30	81	79	79	
100¼	94½	SCM Corp 9¼s90	6	95	95	95	
87⅛	83	SCM Corp 7¼s88	10	87	86½	86[illegible]	

Sample Solution

a. Price of 81 means $810 for each bond.

$810.00	market value
×5	
$4,050.00	cost of 5 bonds
12.50	commission
$4,062.50	Total Cost

b. 5 bonds, $1000 each

$5,000	par value
×.06	
$300.00	Interest

Questions

1. What are the interest rates and due dates of the two Pacific Telephone and Telegraph bonds?
2. a. What is the rate and due date of the Food Fair bond?
   b. What was the closing price?

3. What bonds are owed by Ford Motor Co?

4. What bonds are owed by American Brands?

Problems

1. The price of a 4% bond shown in the newspaper was $75.
   a. What would be the cost of the bond, including a broker's commission of $2.50?
   b. How much interest would the owner receive each year?

2. A 7% bond is listed in the paper at $95, and the broker's commission is $2.50.
   a. What would be the total cost of buying the bond?
   b. How much interest would the owner receive each year?

3. Find the cost, without the broker's fee, of a bond selling at:

a. 103	e. $101\frac{1}{2}$	i. $104\frac{1}{8}$	m. $99\frac{7}{8}$
b. 102	f. $102\frac{3}{4}$	j. $106\frac{3}{8}$	n. $98\frac{7}{8}$
c. $97\frac{1}{2}$	g. $96\frac{1}{8}$	k. $87\frac{5}{8}$	o. $102\frac{5}{8}$
d. $98\frac{1}{4}$	h. $94\frac{5}{8}$	l. $89\frac{5}{8}$	p. $103\frac{5}{8}$

4. Mr. Tompkins bought 10 AT & T $4\frac{3}{8}$s85 at $68\frac{3}{8}$. The broker's commission was $25.
   a. What was the total cost of the bonds?
   b. How much interest will Mr. Tompkins receive yearly?

5. Mr. Stevens bought 10 Gen Motors Acc $6\frac{1}{4}$s88 at $81\frac{1}{8}$. The broker's commission was $25.
   a. What was the cost of the bonds, including commission?
   b. What income will Mr. Stevens receive from the bonds each year?

6. Mr. Orleans bought 5 Penn RR $4\frac{1}{4}$s81 at $63\frac{1}{2}$. Broker's commission was $12.50.
   a. Find the total cost of the bonds.
   b. Find the annual income.

7. Mr. Balter bought 5 Gen Elec 5.30s92 at $75\frac{3}{8}$, and paid brokerage of $12.50.
   a. Find the cost of the bonds.
   b. Find the annual income.

SECTION 5   Finding the Bond Yield

Class Drill

1. Find 6% of $2,000
2. Find 5% of $8,000
3. Find 7% of $5,000
4. Find 8% of $10,000

5. 87×10
6. $103\frac{1}{4} \times 10$
7. $99\frac{3}{4} \times 10$
8. $98\frac{1}{2} \times 10$

9. $102\frac{1}{8} \times 10$
10. $101\frac{3}{8} \times 10$
11. $96\frac{5}{8} \times 10$
12. $97\frac{7}{8} \times 10$

Sample Problem   Mr. Davis owns a 4% Food Fair bond which cost him $680. What rate of return does he earn on his investment? (nearest tenth percent)

Explanation   On page 126 we learned that the market prices of bonds go up or down, depending on various factors, such as current interest rates. In this problem, Food Fair must have issued the 4% bond some years ago when interest rates were lower. Now that interest rates on new bonds are more than 4%, a buyer would not be willing to pay $1,000 for a $1,000 bond that paid only 4%. When the price of the bond drops below $1,000, the effective rate of interest on the bond rises.

Sample Solution

$1,000 par value
  ×.04 rate
$40.00 interest

$$\frac{40}{680} \frac{\text{interest}}{\text{cost}} = \quad .0588 = 5.88\% = 5.9\% \text{ rate}$$

$$680 \overline{)40.00}$$
$$\underline{34\ 00}$$
$$6\ 000$$
$$\underline{5\ 440}$$
$$5600$$

Explanation   In order to find the answer to the nearest tenth percent, solve the division to 4 decimal places.

Another advantage of owning this bond is the gain that will be made when the bond matures. At that time, the owner will receive $1,000 for the bond, although the bond only cost him $680. The difference of $320 is a gain that will be made.

Problems

1. What rate of return will be earned by the owner of a 5% bond that cost $730? (nearest tenth percent)

2. Mr. Horowitz owns a 6% bond that cost him $850. What rate of return does the bond yield? (nearest tenth percent)

3. In each of the following problems, find the yield to the nearest tenth percent.

	Rate	Cost
a)	3%	$550
b)	5%	760
c)	7%	975
d)	$5\frac{1}{2}$%	750
e)	$6\frac{3}{4}$%	960
f)	$7\frac{1}{8}$%	980

4. In the newspaper clipping, there are three 5% bonds of the General Motors Acceptance Corporation. Bonds due in 1977 sold for 82, bonds due in 1980 sold for $76\frac{7}{8}$, and bonds due in 1981 sold for $75\frac{3}{8}$. Why should the 1977 bonds sell for more than bonds maturing at a later date?

5. Find the current yield on these bonds (omit broker's commission):
   a. General Acceptance $9\frac{1}{2}$ s74 at 103
   b. Pac Gas & Elec 3s74 at 82
   c. Ford Motor $8\frac{1}{4}$ s74 at 101
   d. American Brands $5\frac{7}{8}$ s92 at 73
   e. American Can 6s97 at $82\frac{1}{8}$
   f. Am T & T $3\frac{7}{8}$ s90 at 60

UNIT 11

Owning a Home

SECTION 1 Financing Purchase

Class Drill

1. Find 6% of $12,000
2. Find 7% of $14,000
3. Find 5% of $17,000
4. Find $6\frac{1}{2}$% of $15,000
5. Find $5\frac{1}{2}$% of $18,000

6. Divide $30,000 by 15
7. Divide $45,000 by 30
8. Divide $60,000 by 20
9. Divide $25,000 by 15
10. Divide $30,000 by 20

Sample Problem

Mr. Stern bought a home for $34,000. He paid $4,000 as the down payment, and obtained an 8% F.H.A. mortgage for the balance to be paid over the next 30 years. How much must be paid monthly?

Explanation

Most people who buy homes cannot pay cash. Usually the buyer makes a down payment, and obtains a loan from the bank for the balance. As security for the loan, he gives the bank a *mortgage* on his home. If he fails to make payments on the loan, the bank may sell the house in order to obtain money due. The person who borrows and gives the mortgage is called the *mortgagor*, the lender is called the *mortgagee*. In order to obtain the loan, the borrower agrees to pay interest to the lender and to make payments on the loan at regular intervals in order to pay back the money during an agreed upon period of years.

If the home buyer has a good credit record and steady income, and if the house is soundly built, he may be able to obtain an F.H.A. loan. F.H.A. is an abbreviation for the Federal Housing Administration. An F.H.A. loan is a loan obtained from the bank and insured by F.H.A. This insurance protects the bank from loss in the event of failure to repay the loan. As a result, the bank can afford to give better loan terms than it would otherwise be able to give to the borrower. In this way, the F.H.A. helps families buy homes. To pay for this insurance, the F.H.A. charges a premium of 1/2% a year on the average loan balance.

In the sample problem, Mr. Stern owes $30,000 on his mortgage. Since he agreed to pay the loan over 30 years, he would be required to pay $1,000 each year in order to gradually pay back the money he borrowed. His pay-

ment for the first year would therefore be the $1,000 plus interest on $30,000 for one year at 8% or:

$$
\begin{array}{ll}
\text{30,000 Loan} & \text{\$1,000 Payment on Loan} \\
\underline{\times .08} & \underline{\ \ 2,400\ \text{Interest for First Year}} \\
\text{\$2,400.00 Interest} & \text{\$3,400 Payment at end of first year}
\end{array}
$$

For the second year, the interest would be figured on $29,000, the amount he still owes:

$$
\begin{array}{ll}
\text{29,000 Loan} & \text{\$1,000 Payment on Loan} \\
\underline{\times .08} & \underline{\ \ 2,320\ \text{Interest for second year}} \\
\text{\$2,320.00 Interest} & \text{\$3,320 Payment at end of second year}
\end{array}
$$

When the borrower pays part of the loan, he is said to "amortize" the loan. The word "amortization" means the gradual reduction of the amount owed on the mortgage. You can see the yearly payment would gradually decrease, until no further payments were required. However the average home buyer does not wish to make large payments when he first buys his home and small payments later on. He prefers to average the payments and pay the same amount all the time. To do this, payments on the loan are made small at the start when interest payments are high; as interest costs go down, payments on the loan go up, in order to keep the total payment the same.

To find the amount of the monthly payment, the bank uses a table which shows the total payment for the loan and interest. The F.H.A. issues tables which also include the cost of the mortgage insurance. For example, there is this table for an 8% 30-year mortgage:

30 YEARS — 360 MONTHS   **8 PERCENT**

MORTGAGE PRINCIPAL	MONTHLY PAYMENT TO PRINCIPAL & INTEREST	1/12th FIRST ANNUAL PREMIUM	MORTGAGE PRINCIPAL	MONTHLY PAYMENT TO PRINCIPAL & INTEREST	1/12th FIRST ANNUAL PREMIUM	MORTGAGE PRINCIPAL	MONTHLY PAYMENT TO PRINCIPAL & INTEREST	1/12th FIRST ANNUAL PREMIUM	MORTGAGE PRINCIPAL	MONTHLY PAYMENT TO PRINCIPAL & INTEREST	1/12th FIRST ANNUAL PREMIUM	MORTGAGE PRINCIPAL	MONTHLY PAYMENT TO PRINCIPAL & INTEREST	1/12th FIRST ANNUAL PREMIUM
20050	147.17	8.32	24050	176.53	9.98	28050	205.89	11.64	32050	235.25	13.30	36050	264.61	14.96
20100	147.53	8.34	24100	176.89	10.00	28100	206.25	11.66	32100	235.61	13.32	36100	264.97	14.98
20150	147.90	8.36	24150	177.26	10.02	28150	206.62	11.68	32150	235.98	13.34	36150	265.34	15.01
20200	148.27	8.38	24200	177.63	10.05	28200	206.99	11.71	32200	236.35	13.37	36200	265.71	15.03
20250	148.64	8.41	24250	178.00	10.07	28250	207.36	11.73	32250	236.72	13.39	36250	266.08	15.05
20300	149.00	8.43	24300	178.36	10.09	28300	207.72	11.75	32300	237.08	13.41	36300	266.44	15.07
20350	149.37	8.45	24350	178.73	10.11	28350	208.09	11.77	32350	237.45	13.43	36350	266.81	15.09
20400	149.74	8.47	24400	179.10	10.13	28400	208.46	11.79	32400	237.82	13.45	36400	267.18	15.11
20450	150.10	8.49	24450	179.46	10.15	28450	208.82	11.81	32450	238.18	13.47	36450	267.54	15.13
20500	150.47	8.51	24500	179.83	10.17	28500	209.19	11.83	32500	238.55	13.49	36500	267.91	15.15
20550	150.84	8.53	24550	180.20	10.19	28550	209.56	11.85	32550	238.92	13.51	36550	268.28	15.17
20600	151.20	8.55	24600	180.56	10.21	28600	209.92	11.87	32600	239.28	13.53	36600	268.64	15.19
20650	151.57	8.57	24650	180.93	10.23	28650	210.29	11.89	32650	239.65	13.55	36650	269.01	15.21
20700	151.94	8.59	24700	181.30	10.25	28700	210.66	11.91	32700	240.02	13.57	36700	269.38	15.23
20750	152.31	8.61	24750	181.67	10.27	28750	211.03	11.93	32750	240.39	13.59	36750	269.75	15.25
20800	152.67	8.63	24800	182.03	10.29	28800	211.39	11.95	32800	240.75	13.61	36800	270.11	15.28
20850	153.04	8.65	24850	182.40	10.31	28850	211.76	11.98	32850	241.12	13.64	36850	270.48	15.30
20900	153.41	8.68	24900	182.77	10.34	28900	212.13	12.00	32900	241.49	13.66	36900	270.85	15.32
20950	153.77	8.70	24950	183.13	10.36	28950	212.49	12.02	32950	241.85	13.68	36950	271.21	15.34
21000	154.14	8.72	25000	183.50	10.38	29000	212.86	12.04	33000	242.22	13.70	37000	271.58	15.36
21050	154.51	8.74	25050	183.87	10.40	29050	213.23	12.06	33050	242.59	13.72	37050	271.95	15.38
21100	154.87	8.76	25100	184.23	10.42	29100	213.59	12.08	33100	242.95	13.74	37100	272.31	15.40
21150	155.24	8.78	25150	184.60	10.44	29150	213.96	12.10	33150	243.32	13.76	37150	272.68	15.42
21200	155.61	8.80	25200	184.97	10.46	29200	214.33	12.12	33200	243.69	13.78	37200	273.05	15.44
21250	155.98	8.82	25250	185.34	10.48	29250	214.70	12.14	33250	244.06	13.80	37250	273.42	15.46
21300	156.34	8.84	25300	185.70	10.50	29300	215.06	12.16	33300	244.42	13.82	37300	273.78	15.48
21350	156.71	8.86	25350	186.07	10.52	29350	215.43	12.18	33350	244.79	13.84	37350	274.15	15.50
21400	157.08	8.88	25400	186.44	10.54	29400	215.80	12.20	33400	245.16	13.86	37400	274.52	15.52
21450	157.44	8.90	25450	186.80	10.56	29450	216.16	12.22	33450	245.52	13.88	37450	274.88	15.54
21500	157.81	8.92	25500	187.17	10.58	29500	216.53	12.24	33500	245.89	13.91	37500	275.25	15.57
21550	158.18	8.95	25550	187.54	10.61	29550	216.90	12.27	33550	246.26	13.93	37550	275.62	15.59
21600	158.54	8.97	25600	187.90	10.63	29600	217.26	12.29	33600	246.62	13.95	37600	275.98	15.61
21650	158.91	8.99	25650	188.27	10.65	29650	217.63	12.31	33650	246.99	13.97	37650	276.35	15.63
21700	159.28	9.01	25700	188.64	10.67	29700	218.00	12.33	33700	247.36	13.99	37700	276.72	15.65
21750	159.65	9.03	25750	189.01	10.69	29750	218.37	12.35	33750	247.73	14.01	37750	277.09	15.67
21800	160.01	9.05	25800	189.37	10.71	29800	218.73	12.37	33800	248.09	14.03	37800	277.45	15.69
21850	160.38	9.07	25850	189.74	10.73	29850	219.10	12.39	33850	248.46	14.05	37850	277.82	15.71
21900	160.75	9.09	25900	190.11	10.75	29900	219.47	12.41	33900	248.83	14.07	37900	278.19	15.73
21950	161.11	9.11	25950	190.47	10.77	29950	219.83	12.43	33950	249.19	14.09	37950	278.55	15.75
22000	161.48	9.13	26000	190.84	10.79	30000	220.20	12.45	34000	249.56	14.11	38000	278.92	15.77

According to the table, on a $30,000 8%, 30 year mortgage, the borrower must pay $220.20 per month to reduce the principal (the loan) and to pay the interest on the loan, plus $12.45 per month for the F.H.A. mortgage insurance, or a total of $232.65 per month.

Explanation

In the problems that follow you are asked to find yearly payments and yearly interest in order to show how loans are paid off and interest gradually declines. In actual practice, however, payments on mortgages are really paid monthly, based on figures in the table. Both conventional mortgages and F.H.A. mortgages are paid monthly; annual payments are for teaching purposes only.

Problems

1. Mr. Harris bought a home for $32,000. He paid $3,200 down and agreed to pay the balance of $28,800 over the next 30 years, with interest at 8%.
   a. If he agreed to make payments on the loan at the end of each year, what would be the amount of each payment?
   b. If he agreed to pay interest on the unpaid balance of the loan at the end of each year, find the interest for the first year.
   c. Find the balance of the loan at the start of the second year.
   d. Find the interest for the second year.
   e. Find the balance of the loan at the start of the third year.
   f. If he had obtained an F.H.A. mortgage, instead of making annual payments, he would make monthly payments. How much would each monthly payment be? (see table)

2. Mr. Simon bought a home for $33,000. He paid $3,600 down, and signed a 30 year 8% mortgage for the balance of $29,400.
   a. If he agreed to make annual payments on the loan, what would be the amount of each payment?
   b. If he agreed to make annual interest payments, find the interest for the first year.
   c. Find the balance of the loan at the start of the second year.
   d. Find the interest for the second year.
   e. Find the balance of the loan at the start of the third year.
   f. If he had obtained an F.H.A. mortgage, how much would each monthly payment be? (see table)

3. Mr. Evers bought a $24,000 house. He paid $2,000 down, and took a 30 year F.H.A. 8% mortgage for the balance.
   a. Use the table to find his monthly payment for the principal, interest, and F.H.A. insurance.
   b. How much has been paid at the end of one year?
   c. How much has to be paid over 30 years?
   d. How much did he pay, over 30 years, for interest and F.H.A. insurance?

4. Mr. Thompson bought a home for $28,000. He paid $2,600 down, and agreed to a 30-year, F.H.A. 8% mortgage for the balance.
   a. Use the table to find his monthly payment.

b. How much has he paid at the end of one year for amortization, interest, and F.H.A. insurance?

c. How much has he paid over 30 years?

d. How much has he paid over 30 years for interest, and F.H.A. insurance?

SECTION 2   Real Estate Taxes

Class Drill

1. Divide $15,000 by 100
2. Divide $14,300 by 100
3. Divide $17,250 by 100
4. Divide $23,500 by 100

5. Multiply $140 by 3.50
6. Multiply $175 by 5.60
7. Multiply $212 by 6.25
8. Multiply $192 by 5.45

Sample Problems

1. New City estimates that it needs $1,000,000 in real estate taxes during the coming year. If the assessed value of land and buildings subject to tax is $25,000,000, what tax rate should the city set?

2. The tax rate in Old City is $5.25 per $100 of assessed value. What tax must Mr. Jennings pay on his home which is assessed at $22,000?

Explanation

A city estimates what its expenses will be in the coming year. It then decides how much income it will need to meet these expenses. The income is derived from various taxes, such as sales taxes and property taxes. This estimate of income and expense is called the budget.

On each piece of property, the city places a value to be used for tax purposes. This value is called the *assessed value*. The city then decides on a tax rate to be applied to each piece of property, depending on the amount of money it needs. To do this, the city divides the amount of real estate taxes needed by the total assessed value of real estate, and expresses the answer as a decimal or as a rate for each $100 of property.

Sample Solutions

Problem 1.

$$\frac{1,000,000 \text{ Tax}}{25,000,000 \text{ Value of Property}} = \frac{1}{25} = .04 \text{ or } 4\% \text{ or } \$4 \text{ per } \$100$$

Problem 2.

$22,000 divided by 100 = 220 hundreds

$$
\begin{array}{r}
220 \text{ Hundreds} \\
\times 5.25 \text{ Rate per } \$100 \\
\hline
1,100 \\
440 \\
1100 \\
\hline
\$1,155.00 \text{ Tax}
\end{array}
$$

Problems

1. The assessed value of Mr. Donald's house is $15,000. If the tax rate is $4 per $100, how much must he pay?

2. The assessed value of George Benton's house is $18,000. If the tax rate is $5 per $100, how much real estate tax must he pay?

3. In each of the following problems find the real property tax:

	Assessed Value	Tax Rate
a.	$12,000	$4.50 per $100
b.	14,000	5.75 per $100
c.	21,000	4.65 per $100
d.	23,000	5.25 per $100
e.	24,500	4.32 per $100
f.	23,400	5.13 per $100

4. In a certain city the assessed value of property is 60% of its market value. If the tax rate is $5 per $100, find the tax on property worth $15,000.

5. In Central City, the assessed value of property is 60% of its true value. If the tax rate is $4 per $100, find the real estate tax on property worth $25,000.

6. A city estimates that it will need to collect $5,000,000 in real estate taxes. If the assessed value of property in the city totals $100,000,000, what should its tax rate be?

7. A city has assessed real property of $75,000,000. If it wishes to collect $3,000,000 in real estate taxes, find the tax rate.

SECTION 3   Cost of Maintenance

Class Drill

1. Find 2% of $23,000

2. Find 3% of $25,000

3. Find 2% of $18,500

4. Find 2% of $17,500

5. Find 6% of $15,000

6. Find 7% of $23,000

7. Find 6% of $19,400

8. Find 8% of $16,700

Sample Problem

Mr. Mason rents his home for $300 a month. He could buy the house for $25,000 by putting $5,000 down and paying the balance subject to a 7% mortgage, over 20 years. As an owner, his expenses for the first year would be: real estate taxes $1,000; insurance $100; fuel $250; repairs $125; depre-

135

ciation of house, 2% of $19,000 (the value of the building, aside from the land); interest on the mortgage 7% of $20,000.

    a) If Mr. Mason decides to buy the house, how much would it cost him to maintain it for the first year?

    b) If Mr. Mason could have kept his $5,000 down payment in the savings bank at 5%, would it be cheaper to buy or rent the house? How much cheaper?

Explanation

The owner of a house must consider the following expenses:

    a) Interest on the unpaid amount of the mortgage must be paid. We learned previously that monthly payments are usually made to reduce the amount of the mortgage, and thus the interest payments are gradually reduced. In these problems we shall assume that the mortgage payment will be made at the end of the first year, so that calculations will be based on the full amount of the mortgage in order to find the interest expense for the first year.

    b) The real estate tax, based on the tax rate and the assessed valuation, must be paid.

    c) Insurance must be purchased on the home to protect against fire loss and other possible losses.

    d) Fuel must be purchased for heat and hot water.

    e) Money must be used to pay for repairs, painting, and other maintenance expenses.

    f) As the home becomes older, it will depreciate and gradually lose value (except during periods of inflation). This depreciation is an expense of owning a house. The depreciation does not, of course, apply to the land.

    g) A final consideration, though not an actual expense to be paid, is the loss of interest that could have been earned in a savings bank if the house had not been bought.

Sample Solution

a)

$20,000	Mortgage
.07	Interest rate
$1,400.00	Interest for first year

$19,000	House
.02	Dep. rate
$380.00	Depreciation

$1,400.	Interest on mortgage
1,000.	Real estate taxes
100.	Insurance
250.	Fuel
125.	Repairs
380.	Depreciation of house
3,255.	Expenses for first year

b)

$5,000.	Savings
.05	Interest rate
$250.00	Interest lost

$3,255	Costs
250	Lost interest
3,505.	Total cost

$300	Rent per month
12	
$3,600	Rent per year

$3,600.	Rent per year
3,505.	Cost of owning a house
$ 95.	Saving for first year

136

Problems

1. If Mr. Apple buys a home, his expenses for the first year would be:

   7% interest on $10,000 mortgage
   2% depreciation on house valued at $11,000 (aside from land)
   $600 real estate taxes
   $ 85 insurance
   $135 Fuel
   $ 60 Repairs

   a) Find the total expense for the first year.
   b) Mr. Apple would have to make a $5,000 down payment, which now earns 5% interest in the savings bank. Would it be cheaper to buy or rent, if he can rent the house for $200 a month?

2. Mr. Briggs would like to buy a home. His expenses for the first year would be:

   8% interest on $12,000 mortgage
   3% depreciation on $9,000 house
   $500 real estate taxes
   $110 Insurance
   $140 Fuel
   $75 Repairs

   a) Find the total expense for the first year.
   b) Mr. Briggs would have to make a $3,000 down payment. He now has this money in a savings bank earning 5% interest. Would it be cheaper to buy or rent, if he can rent the house for $225 a month?

3. In each of the following problems find whether it would be cheaper to own the house or rent it for the first year.

Yearly Costs of Owning the House

	Rental Monthly	Int. on Mortgage	Depreciation	Taxes	Insurance	Fuel	Repairs	Lost Savings Interest
a)	$250	7% of $14,000	2% of $1,500	$650	$125	$145	$75	5% of $4,000
b)	150	6% of 9,000	2% of 8,000	475	90	120	60	5% of 3,000
c)	150	6% of 11,000	2% of 10,000	420	80	100	45	5% of 4,000
d)	250	7% of 15,000	2% of 14,000	740	130	145	90	5% of 4,000

4. Mr. Eggers owns a two family house. His yearly expenses are as follows:

   $1,500 interest
   480 depreciation
   1,500 real estate taxes
   170 insurance
   280 fuel
   140 repairs

   a) Find the yearly cost.
   b) Mr. Eggers rents an apartment to a tenant for $250 a month. What does it cost Mr. Eggers per month to live in his own apartment?

5. Mr. Duffy owns his two family house. His yearly expenses are as follows:

$1,400 interest on mortgage
   430 depreciation

      1,600 real estate taxes
       160 insurance
       250 fuel
       150 repairs

a) Find the yearly cost.
b) If Mr. Duffy rents an apartment to a tenant for $200 a month, what does Mr. Duffy's apartment cost him each month?

SECTION 4   Review Problems Units X, XI: Stocks and Bonds, Owning a Home

1. Mr. Hampton bought 100 shares of American Telephone stock at $44, and paid a commission of $56. At a later date he sold the stock at 51, paid a commission of $60 to his broker, and paid $5 in transfer taxes.
   a. What was the total cost of the stock?
   b. How much cash did Mr. Hampton receive when he sold the stock?
   c. What was his profit or loss?

2. Mr. James owns 100 shares of Monarch Corporation stock, which he purchased for $17\frac{1}{4}$ a share, plus a commission to the broker of $52. At a later date he sold the stock at $18\frac{5}{8}$, paid a commission of $54 to his broker, and paid transfer taxes of $5.
   a. What was the total cost of the stock?
   b. How much cash did he receive at the time of sale?
   c. What was his profit or loss?

3. Mr. Foster received a quarterly dividend of $.60 last year on his Mobil Oil stock. He owns 100 shares of the stock.
   a. How much did he receive in dividends for the year?
   b. If he paid $4,000 for the stock, what was his annual rate of return on his investment?

4. Mr. Kaufman received dividends on his stock totaling $75 for the year. If the stock cost him $1,545, what percent did he earn on his investment? (to the nearest percent)

5. Mr. Gladstone bought 10 Philadelphia Electric bonds, interest rate 8%, at $99\frac{1}{2}$, and paid brokerage of $25.
   a. What was the total cost of the bonds?
   b. How much interest will Mr. Gladstone receive each year?

6. Mr. O'Neill owns General Motors Acceptance Corporation bonds which cost him $825 each. The bonds pay 5% interest. What rate of return does he earn on his investment? (find answer to nearest tenth percent).

7. The real estate tax rate in a certain city is $5.40 per $100 of assessed value. If Mr. Salmon owns a home assessed at $23,000, how much real estate tax must he pay?

8. After Mr. Samuels owned his home for one year, he figured his expenses were:

> 7% interest on his $14,000 mortgage
> 2% depreciation on the house valued at $15,000,
>   aside from the value of the land
> $650 real estate taxes
> $125 insurance
> $150 fuel
> $110 repairs

   a. Find the total expense for the first year.
   b. Mr. Samuels paid a $5,000 down payment. He used to keep this money in a savings bank paying 5% interest. He no longer earns this interest. He used to pay rent of $260 a month. Is it cheaper to rent the house or to own it?

9. Mr. Travers bought a home for $32,000. He paid $5,000 down, and signed a 30 year 7% mortgage for the balance.
   a. Assuming he amortized the mortgage only at the end of each year, what would be the amount paid at the end of the first year for the mortgage payment?
   b. What would the interest be for the first year, if paid at the end of the year?
   c. Find the balance of the loan at the start of the second year.
   d. Find the interest for the second year.